Gordon Cressy
Tells Great Stories

Gordon Cressy
Tells Great
Stories

Gordon Cressy

IGUANA

Publisher: Cheryl Hawley
Editor: Cheryl Hawley
Front cover design: Jonathan Relph

ISBN 978-1-77180-670-1 (paperback)

This is an original print edition of *Gordon Cressy Tells Great Stories*.

To my mom and dad, Joe and Sybil Cressy, who gave me solid values, who supported me when I chose a different path, and even canvassed for me, for the NDP in Rosedale!

To my amazing children, Jennifer, Jillian, Joseph, and Keith, who each in their own way is working to make this world a better place.

To my grandchildren in the United States, Kyle, Ella, and Olivia, it is such a privilege watching you grow up, although mostly at a distance, and sharing special times at the cottage each summer.

To my Toronto grandchildren, Teddy and Jude, having you in our lives every day has given Joanne and me more joy than we can ever express.

To Joanne, you have lit up my life for over forty years. Your brilliant strategic mind and your wise counsel have been fundamental to every move I have made. You are the rock and the nurturer of our whole family. Together we have shared a most excellent adventure. And there is more yet to come. My love for you is forever.

"All men dream, but not equally. Those who dream by night in the dusty recesses of their mind, wake in the day to find that it was vanity: but the dreamers of the day are dangerous men, for they may act on their dreams with open eyes, to make them possible."

— T. E. Lawrence, *Seven Pillars of Wisdom*

"Trials never end, of course. Unhappiness and misfortune are bound to occur as long as people live, but there is a feeling now, that was not here before, and is not just on the surface of things, but penetrates all the way through: We've won it. It is going to get better now. You can sort of tell these things."

— Robert M. Pirsig, *Zen and the Art of Motorcycle Maintenance*

"Make no little plans. They have no magic to stir men's blood.... Make big plans, aim high in hope and work..."

—Daniel Burnham, *Plan of Chicago*, 1909

Table of Contents

Preface

Gordon Cressy is a walking, talking civics lesson.

He is a crash course in humanity. That grin, that burst of warmth, and he has got you.

But first, a story:

The tale of a young man from Lawrence Park Collegiate is really the story of modern-day Toronto.

Or, how Toronto became, well, Toronto the Good.

He is not responsible completely for that of course — but the place is immeasurably better for his larger-than-life presence.

I know of no better community builder on the planet. Cressy's work is the connective tissue that makes Toronto — the city that takes top spots globally in livability rankings for diversity, inclusivity, and tolerance — what it is today.

After reading one seemingly impossible story after the other, I had forgotten just how many roads lead to Gordon. Few know just how many lives he has had or the immense behind-the-scenes contributions he has made to the fabric of Canadian society.

Gordon's voice — clear, self-deprecating, ever optimistic — is in every sentence. It is practically an audiobook. I can hear that timbre still in my head as I turn the pages.

From his work with business titans such as Jack Cockwell, Allan Slaight, and Martha Billes, to religious figures such as Cardinal Emmett

Carter, to political titans such as Nelson Mandela (with a stop along with way for dinner with the Ugandan dictator Idi Amin), Cressy has been a witness to and enthusiastic instigator of some of the most historic events in Toronto's history.

His hand has been nearly invisible but immensely impactful in ways big and small.

There was the time he was involved in getting South African President Nelson Mandela to speak to 50,000 students at the SkyDome. Or, as the CEO of the Learning Partnership, when he created Take Our Kids to Work Day, which more than a quarter million students participate in each year.

There were the changes he made as the head of the United Way, diversifying the organization to represent what the city truly looked like, including getting community activist Dr. Joseph Wong to forge a new way forward.

Gordon's foray into the private sector led him to help create, launch, and implement Canadian Tire's nationally recognized signature programme, Jump Start.

But that is just a sampling. Along the way, countless lives have been changed for the better.

While the book unfolds as a fish-out-of-water tale of a kid from North Toronto ending up in the Caribbean and transforming lives, including his own, it is also a story about youth and growing up. It is a story about giving. But it is ultimately the story of the people who made Toronto the community it is today.

(His tale is not limited to Canada. There are important footprints left behind in Trinidad and Tobago, where he headed up the YMCA; Chicago, where he was a youth worker on the city's south side at the height of the civil rights movement; and China, where he created his own kind of ping-pong diplomacy.)

But that is just the globe-trotting stuff. The stuff that forged him. When he got back home, Toronto was never the same.

To some who do not know his legacy, Gordon Cressy is the auctioneer at black-tie functions. He might be charming a billionaire or two to buy the gloves of a former heavyweight champion or convincing a musical superstar to sing for a $10,000 donation.

But there is so much more in between. I am glad he got these stories on paper because he does tell great stories.

My favourite should really have been a movie. And, at one point, it almost was. Fresh out of Toronto, he ended up becoming the general secretary of the YMCA in Trinidad at the age of nineteen. And there, he raised — with a lot of difficulty and immense chutzpah — a record amount of money for the organization selling, of all things, Canadian Christmas trees to residents on the tropical island. Because, well, he's Gordon Cressy.

And that is pretty much what he has been doing since. Selling dreams. And, more importantly, making them happen.

— Tony Wong, Contributing Columnist, *Toronto Star*

Introduction

For many years I was in demand as a public speaker. I spoke at conferences and workshops across Canada and a few times in the United States and the Caribbean.

Mostly I told stories about my experiences and reflected on lessons I had learned. My sons, Joseph and Keith, and my wife, Joanne, encouraged me to write down many of these stories, which they had heard for years. The Covid pandemic gave me the time to get to work.

First off, this is not an autobiography. Rather it is a collection of stories based on work I have done, places I have been, experiences I have had, and things I have learned. Sometimes I have been part of the action, sometimes I have had a front-row seat, and sometimes I have watched from afar. Mostly, though, I have been a participant and not a spectator. I like it that way.

Most of the stories are true as I remember them. A couple are exaggerated, and one, I made up completely. I fess up in the telling.

This book does not speak to my early years. I grew up in North Toronto, went to Bedford Park School, Lawrence Park Collegiate, and Northern Secondary School, attended St. Leonard's Church, sang in the choir, did Cubs and Scouts, and was then and am now part of a wonderful family. It is an important story too, but for another time.

What follows then is quite a journey. It starts in Trinidad, heads to Chicago, comes to Toronto for a long time, wends its way back to Trinidad and Tobago, and now ends up back in Toronto. There are stops along the way that include Africa and China. Thanks for joining me on the ride.

And it is not over yet.

— Gordon Cressy, October 2023

Going to Trinidad
Listen and Learn

It was March Break of 1963. While taking the Ryerson business course at Northern Secondary, I got a job working for that week as a janitor at the school. I saw a poster on the wall that said: "Plenty of Work in the Caribbean — No Pay." I was intrigued. I applied and, to my surprise, was accepted by the Canadian Voluntary Commonwealth Services (which merged shortly thereafter with the Canadian University Service Overseas, CUSO, the equivalent of the U.S. Peace Corps).

In June 1963, twenty of us showed up for a one-day orientation session at Hart House at the University of Toronto. My friend and neighbour Paul Follett and I were the youngest; most were university graduates. I wound up being assigned to work with the YMCA in Trinidad. I remember little of the orientation save for one powerful lesson. Austin Clarke, the brilliant author originally from Barbados, was leading the orientation. He looked at each of us in turn and asked, "So why are you going?"

The question was troubling for me as I had applied on a bit of a lark.

I knew I could not mention the idea of beautiful beaches (I mean, I had never even been on an airplane!) — so I relied on my church background and said something like, "I am going to help the people."

Austin Clarke shot back, "If you are going to help the people, don't bother!" Then he followed up with this zinger: "If you are going to listen and learn, then you might be able to help the people." Wise words indeed. Some twenty-five years on I met up with Austin Clarke and thanked him.

Before leaving for Trinidad, I met a remarkable YMCA staff person, Bob Torrance, who took me under his wing. He suggested that, since I was a good swimmer, I should take my Water Safety Instructor course at the Toronto YMCA and become certified to teach swimming. I did just that. My other athletic skill was in table tennis, where I had won the Ontario Junior title that year. I had no idea whether people in Trinidad played table tennis.

In late August, at age nineteen, accompanied to the airport by my parents and two brothers, I flew on my own to Port of Spain, Trinidad, arriving in the early evening. No one was at the airport to meet me. I was in a new country and felt very alone. Growing up in Toronto I had never met anyone who was not white, except at the Moonglow — the local Chinese restaurant.

I somehow figured out how to use the phone and called the YMCA and reached the other Canadian there, Dennis McDermott. He said they thought I was coming the following week, so he told me just to take a taxi.

The YMCA was in the heart of Port of Spain at 16-17 Victoria Square, a grand old house that had been converted into many individual rooms and functioned as a hostel. Sometimes tourists stayed there, but it housed mainly students and working men. I was thrilled to discover a couple of table-tennis tables out back!

The early days were times of great learning. The second night there I was excited to discover that there was a radio station from the U.S. military base on the island that broadcast NHL hockey games. I had just settled in to listen to the Toronto Maple Leafs play the New York Rangers when Bing Mandbodh, one of the residents who passed away a couple of years ago, burst into my room and asked what I was doing. I told him how excited I was to be able to listen to a hockey game. He turned off the radio and said to me, "You did not come to Trinidad to listen to hockey games."

Off we went to watch Trinidadians play one of their favourite sports—cricket. We drank a couple of cold Carib beers and I ate my first roti (a favourite food in Trinidad). A neat beginning.

Playing table tennis gave me credibility with the local kids right at the start. I was not the best player but I was competitive, and it helped me to make friends quickly. It also helped me to understand and learn the wonderful Trinidadian accent. We formed a YMCA team and played in the C Division of the Port of Spain league. I even won the B Division Singles city championship.

Things at the Y changed quickly. The only other Canadian, Dennis McDermott, soon left to work in Guyana. Shortly after that, Derek Gardiner, the general secretary of the Trinidad YMCA, returned to work with the Y in England.

The steering committee of the YMCA was made up mainly of men of influence in Trinidad. The chair of the committee, Dennis Mahabir (who was the mayor of Port of Spain), announced that I was the new general secretary of the YMCA. Unbelievable! I was nineteen ... I could teach swimming and play table tennis and was enthusiastic ... but that was about it.

The title did not work for the residents of the hostel or our kids.

They had started to call me Gordon the Warden, and the title stuck.

I discovered if we sent in four Kellogg's Corn Flakes box tops and US$2, I could get a licence-plate sign with the name WARDEN on it. A couple of weeks later, the sign arrived and we nailed it to the office door.

Looking back, that was the moment I had to grow up and grow up fast.

The hostel kind of ran itself, with Thelma and Carole, the cooks, and Sylvie, who made the rooms neat and tidy. I learned to purchase food at the market and how to haggle for a better price.

But I now had to run a YMCA youth programme. It was sink or swim.

I chose to swim.

Gone Swimming — But Where?

I discovered that there were no beaches near Port of Spain, and most young people living there, in fact most people, did not know how to swim. Given the YMCA's history in aquatics, I suggested to the steering committee that we should look at teaching kids to swim. The only places with swimming pools were the hotels and some villas with wealthy owners. So off I went to the nearest hotel, Bretton Hall, and pitched them on the idea of having our YMCA kids use the pool a couple of days a week. They listened politely and then informed me in no uncertain terms that their pool was for hotel guests only. It was very clear that the other hotels would say the same thing. I came back to the steering committee and we discussed options.

A couple of the members remembered a pool, long out of use, down by the harbour that had been built by the U.S. during the Second World War. We went down to meet with the Harbour Commission. They said we could lease the pool for $1 per year on the basis that all expenses related to the pool would be paid by the YMCA.

Off we went to see the pool. It was large but dirty, with muck everywhere, and it had no filtration system. We were not deterred. The kids cleaned up the pool. We got special pool paint donated and painted the pool. One of our steering committee members knew Alfred Drax, the head of the fire department, who agreed to fill the pool with water. I am not sure how it all happened, but two weeks later, we formally opened the pool with lots of media attention!

Each week the fire department put 80,000 gallons of water in the pool. We added chlorine, and once a week the fire service would drain the pool and then pump in another 80,000 gallons. This worked great for the first six months. Then I think someone at the fire department asked how this cost fit into the budget. Very soon we were looking for an alternative.

Not far from the Y pool was the Trinidad and Tobago Electricity Commission. Flowing from there was a narrow hot-and-cold stream that went all the way to the sea, passing by the Y pool. Someone suggested we divert part of the stream to fill the pool and then let it exit to the sea. Amazingly it worked!

The Learn to Swim programme flourished, and over the years the YMCA obtained a state-of-the-art filtration system and developed other programmes on that site. Eventually the hostel closed, and the expanded pool site became the Y headquarters, with a range of other activities, including basketball, daycare, and a variety of adult and youth programmes.

Today over 150,000 Trinidadians have learned to swim at the YMCA. Many other pools have been built, and competitive swimming has grown enormously, producing Olympic-level swimmers.

Some forty-five years later, my wife Joanne and I returned to the sister island of Tobago, where we lived for three years and worked with the local community to build the first-ever YMCA facility. We did a needs assessment when we arrived, and it was clear that what people wanted most was a public swimming pool. This time though we had to start from scratch — but that is another story, which I will get to later.

Selling Christmas Trees in Trinidad

Now that I was the general secretary, I had to learn many new things, like balancing a budget. I learned very fast when it became clear that we were spending more money than we were bringing in. It certainly was not my salary, which was TT$10 per week. We could not raise the room rate or meal cost. It was suggested that we try to raise some money. Although I have spent a good part of the last thirty years in fundraising, back then I knew precious little.

I tried to remember what had worked growing up in Toronto. I remembered that our local church, St. Leonard's, used to raise money selling Christmas trees. I went to the steering committee and suggested if we sold Christmas trees there would be no competition. One member asked if I had developed a business plan. Heck, I did not even know what a business plan was!

I have learned over the years that bold and exciting ideas excite. Several steering committee members had visited Canada at Christmastime and thought the idea just might work.

I got the go-ahead and contacted the YMCA in St. John, New Brunswick, which sourced 1,500 Scotch pine trees for us and put them on a cargo ship. The ship operators told us the trees would arrive on December 15, nice and fresh. Our boys at the Y went out and presold 1,200 trees. This story was gaining traction. There was a little article in the newspaper — my name was in it. I sent it home to my mom and dad. My mom shared it with her bridge club group!

Everything was going very smoothly until our trees did not arrive as promised on December 15. We did not make many long-distance calls in those days, but I sure did that day. I called the Y folks who said there had been a "small" fire on the ship. The trees had been put on another ship and were scheduled to arrive December 22. I remember saying, "Wow, that's really close to Christmas." They suggested we call the port authority in Bermuda and find out how the ship was progressing. We learned, to our horror, that there was a dockworkers' strike in Bermuda, and now the trees would arrive in Barbados on December 22, but would not get to Trinidad until after Christmas! Things were going quickly from bad to worse, and the enthusiasm and support for this young Canadian volunteer was diminishing at a rapid rate.

My suggestion of changing the date of Christmas did not go down very well, especially with the clergy! One of the steering committee members, Steve Hanuman, knew the head of British West Indian Airways (now Caribbean Airlines) quite well. The next morning off we went to BWIA and suggested to them an innovative marketing opportunity in which they would give the YMCA a cargo plane. We would fly over to Grantley Adams Airport in Barbados, go down to the docks, take the trees off the ship, load them onto some trucks, drive out to the airport, and stuff those trees on the plane. We would then fly back to Piarco Airport in Trinidad, take the trees off the plane, load them on the trucks, drive down to the YMCA, and sell those trees. Lo and behold, they agreed! There was a headline in a Trinidad newspaper: "Christmas Tree Airlift to Raise Funds for YMCA!"

On December 22, steering committee members James Dube and Frank Mohan, my friend Bing Mandbodh and I, a couple of flight attendants, and the pilot, plus a few bottles of Old Oak Rum (a very fine Trinidadian rum), flew out in the early morning for Barbados. We got down to the dockside to discover that, it being a Sunday, the dockworkers were not working — but a few of the workers were hanging around. A few bottles of Trinidadian rum later they were working, and together we loaded the trees onto the trucks, drove to the airport, and stuffed those trees into every nook and cranny on the plane. Mr. Bal Soochit, a YMCA volunteer in Trinidad, donated the trucks both in Barbados and Trinidad.

We flew back to Trinidad in the late afternoon, took the trees off the plane, loaded them onto the trucks, and drove down to the YMCA in Port of Spain. There was a festive atmosphere when we arrived, with Christmas carols blasting on the radio. Trinidad's TV station covered the arrival. We started selling right away. Families came by that night to buy trees, and for the next two days we sold trees nonstop. By Christmas Eve we had sold out! We were tired but very pleased. We turned a bad situation into a wonderful ending. People had their trees. The media loved the story, and we had raised about TT$7,000.

On Christmas Day, we were having lunch at the Y and I mentioned that it just would not be Christmas without a Christmas tree, to which one of our residents chimed in with the fact that Jesus was born under olive trees and not Christmas trees. On December 28, the Trinidad government banned the mass importation of trees, suggesting that people grow local trees.

That should have been the end of the story, but not quite. About thirty years ago, Douglas Bain, a middle-aged man from Trinidad, showed up at the University of Toronto, where I was working, and told me that I had taught him how to swim at the Y in Trinidad. Not only that, he mentioned that he helped sell those Christmas trees. He said he and his buddy had gotten tired of selling the trees and threw twenty of them over the back fence. Then they went down to the corner and sold them and made $200. Obviously, a little private entrepreneurial experience.

Loading the plane in Barbados.

With my friend Paul Follet.

A decade ago, Stuart McLean of the popular *Vinyl Café* radio show on CBC, asked if he could tell the Christmas tree story on the radio. Not being one to shy away from publicity, I readily agreed. The story played across the country, and I got a few emails from old friends. On the following Monday, I got a long-distance call from a Zale Dalen in BC, who told me that he was a movie producer and he thought this Christmas tree story would be a great feature film. Much like *Cool Runnings* about the Jamaican bobsled team — but in reverse. I was excited. I was already thinking of who would play the male lead. I rushed home to tell my wife, Joanne, about this upcoming blockbuster film. She looked at me a bit skeptically and said, "I am not sure this movie will ever be made." Well, she was right, the movie never got made, but the story lingers on.

In November 2013, the *Trinidad Guardian* wrote a feature about the Christmas tree story on its fiftieth anniversary. A few years ago, I received the following remarkable email from Tony Mark Ramjewan (quoted with permission from the author).

From: Tony Ramjewan
To: Gordon Cressy
Sent: Thursday, April 21, 2016 9:28 AM
Subject: Attn Gordon Cressy's Trinidad and Tobago. Story's I here about u

As a kid my mom and grand mother use to tell me stories of a young man who came to Trinidad to work in the ymca to be 1963 my mom was only 6 years old but she said my grand ma had buy a pine Christmas tree from you she could still remember the smell of pine my grand mother said she would never forget your smile and how gentle you was. she pay 18 dollar for her tree. She even told me knowing u was in the ymca she would some time drop off food for u. U being. A teen in a strange island.. I always here that name every Christmas Gordon Cressy the young man who change Christmas in Trinidad. Every Christmas all my family would get together and my grand ma would tell us about her first real tree and the young man that help her and the troubles u went true to get them tree to Trinidad one being the cargo ship being on fire but the trees being save and put on a next ship but that port was close. And then being stuck in Barbados bwia help u. On December 22 u get the trees I just wanted to thank you for brining that joy to my family and the tradition of my grand ma telling us your story every Christmas morning She been telling your story every Christmas morning till she pass away 2003.

Thank you again.

Official Opening Trinidad YMCA, April 6, 1964

During my first few months in Trinidad, the YMCA was governed by a steering committee of influential Trinidadians. The plan was to develop a constitution, create a board of directors, and be formally recognized by the World Alliance of YMCAs in Geneva, Switzerland.

This all came together on April 6, 1964, on our YMCA grounds.

A large crowd came for the event, including religious and community leaders, politicians, the media, and a good number of our Y kids. It was an exciting time.

We were thrilled to have the chief justice, Sir Hugh Wooding, address the crowd. My minimal role at the event was to read greetings from the YMCA in Barbados, Jamaica, Canada, and the World Alliance in Switzerland. The media picture below shows me speaking. It should have been Sir Hugh Wooding.

I found out later that Chester Morong, a resident at our YMCA and a reporter at the *Mirror* newspaper, arranged this. I asked him why he did it. He said, "Sir Hugh is in the media all the time. This will impress your parents back in Canada." He was right!

● Mr. Gordon Cressy, acting general secretary (standing) reads messages from outside organisations at the inaugural meeting yesterday. Others in picture are Mr. Harry Farrell (extreme left) Sir Hugh Wooding, Mr. Dennis Mahabir and Mr. Frank Mohan.

'YMCA A MEANS TO FIGHT ILLS'

THE Young Men Christian Association (YMCA) is a means of fighting the ills that exist in this country, the Chief Justice Sir Hugh Wooding said yesterday afternoon.

Sir Hugh was addressing a large gathering at the inauguration ceremony of officers of the Port-of-Spain YMCA, on Ariapita Avenue.

"YMCAs should resolve to practise their motto which is "That they may all be be one," he said.

Sir Hugh is one of the association's honorary presidents.

He hoped that the new officers would undertake work in order to make the underprivileged feel that they stand on some sort of equality.

"I trust that the officers will appreciate the measure of opportunity and the extent of their work and so fulfil the task undertaken," he added.

After the opening prayer by Rev. A. N. MacKean, Mr. Dennis Mahabir, president, told the gathering that he saw the occasion as a reward long and patiently awaited.

The members inaugurated were Mr. Dennis Mahabir, president; and Bishop William J. Hughes, Sir Hugh Wooding, Sir Lindsay Grant, honorary presidents.

Mr. Frank Mohan, vice-president; and Mr. Harry Farrell, recording secretary, Mr. Louis Blache-Fraser, treasurer; and Mr. Gordon Cressy, acting general secretary.

d by Trinidad Mirror Newspapers Limited, 62-68 Richmon

APRIL 1964

Did Not Get That One Right

Sometimes my naive enthusiasm led to bad judgement. One Friday I was meeting with the local bank manager. To impress, I wore my blue blazer with a YMCA Canada crest on it. I also wore a pair of glasses with window-pane lenses to make me look older. After the meeting, I was walking down the street when a man approached me. He said he worked for a wealthy Canadian woman who thought she recognized me. He asked if I was from Toronto or Montreal. I told him Toronto. He said, then she knows you from Toronto. I was impressed. He said that she would like to invite me to her house for a swim in her pool and dinner. I was excited but said I did not have a swimsuit. He said she had extras or we could swim in the nude! Now this was getting exciting! He said, "Let's get in a taxi and go there now." I thought for a moment and realized that I would miss table tennis, but this was an opportunity not to be missed. So we got in the cab and drove off. After a couple of minutes, we stopped at the local rum shop. He said it would be a nice idea if I brought her a bottle of rum as a gift. I thought this was a swell idea and gave him $10. Some ten minutes later, he was still not back. I waited and waited and waited. Finally, the taxi driver turned to me and said, "He is not coming back." I had been had. I paid the taxi driver and walked back to the YMCA. In the end, I did make it for table-tennis class — and learned the well-known lesson … if it sounds too good to be true it probably is.

It Is Always Hard to Say Goodbye

One day at the YMCA in Port of Spain, I got a call from the U.S. Consulate asking if we would like two well-known family-life educators, Dr. Sylvanus Duvall and Dr. Evelyn Duvall, to visit our Y and talk to our young members. Dr. Evelyn Duvall had written a book entitled *Facts of Life and Love for Teen-Agers*, which I had read in high school. Seemed like a good idea, I thought. They came and chatted a bit with our young people. To be honest, I do not think they made much impact at all.

After the kids left, we talked. It turned out that Dr. Sylvanus Duvall was a professor at George Williams College in Chicago (George Williams was the founder of the YMCA in England). He suggested that I come to study there. Next thing I knew, I had a scholarship and later that year moved into residence at George Williams College at 5200 Drexel Avenue on the south side of Chicago. The tuition was $500 per year.

I was now on a new path, and it was time to leave Trinidad. The board gave me a nice send-off party, which the press covered. I attended the Canada Day celebration and met Dr. Eric Williams, who was prime minister of Trinidad and Tobago.

But it was saying goodbye to the kids and my fellow residents that tore at my heart. That year had changed my life forever — although I did not know it at the time.

This was my new family, who had welcomed me in and had taught me to dream big.

On the last night, I was with my friends Bing Manbodh and Norman Mohan. We drank way too much, but I do remember this. Norman turned to me and said, "Don't forget us and come back soon." I, of course, said I would. Norman passed away many years ago, and Bing sadly passed away a couple of years ago. Looking back, that time in Trinidad changed my life path forever. I had grown up to believe I would be a businessman. Now community service had become my passion.

Over the years I found ways to return to Trinidad many times. Still do.

Before I left, the chair of the YMCA, Dennis Mahabir, wrote a reference letter for me. I like it a lot. I never used it, but I saved it all these years.

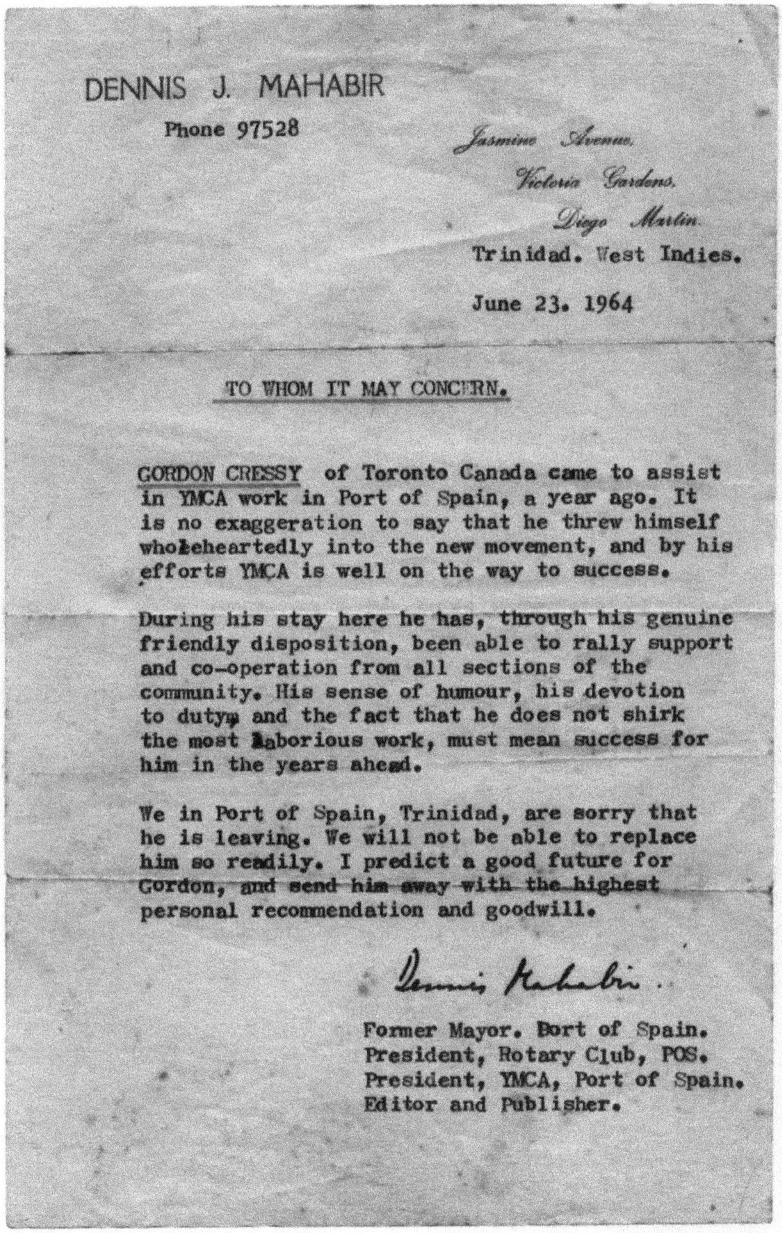

DENNIS J. MAHABIR

Phone 97528

Jasmine Avenue,

Victoria Gardens.

Diego Martin.

Trinidad. West Indies.

June 23. 1964

TO WHOM IT MAY CONCERN.

GORDON CRESSY of Toronto Canada came to assist
in YMCA work in Port of Spain, a year ago. It
is no exaggeration to say that he threw himself
wholeheartedly into the new movement, and by his
efforts YMCA is well on the way to success.

During his stay here he has, through his genuine
friendly disposition, been able to rally support
and co-operation from all sections of the
community. His sense of humour, his devotion
to duty, and the fact that he does not shirk
the most laborious work, must mean success for
him in the years ahead.

We in Port of Spain, Trinidad, are sorry that
he is leaving. We will not be able to replace
him so readily. I predict a good future for
Gordon, and send him away with the highest
personal recommendation and goodwill.

Dennis Mahabir.

Former Mayor. Port of Spain.
President, Rotary Club, POS.
President, YMCA, Port of Spain.
Editor and Publisher.

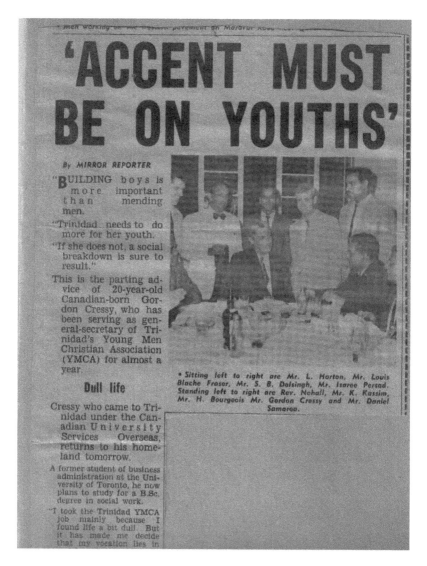

Going-away party, July 1964.

Let's Go Camping

I was midway through my first year at George Williams College (the YMCA training school) in Chicago. It was bitterly cold, and I missed my friends in Trinidad. Teaching kids swimming in Chicago was nothing like the warm water in the YMCA pool in Port of Spain.

I wrote a letter to Dennis Mahabir, the chair of the YMCA, and suggested that the Y organize a summer camp. My further, somewhat manipulative, idea was to have the Trinidad Y request that the Canadian YMCA send Gordon Cressy down to run the camp. They agreed, and another young Canadian, Eric Bojesen, and I arrived in Port of Spain on a Wednesday night. The Y board told us there was a press conference on Thursday to talk about the camp, which was to start the following Monday. But in Trini fashion, we had no location for the camp, no kids registered, and no staff hired. Unbelievable.

But also in Trini fashion, we did open on Monday with forty kids!

We got a school donated in Carenage. Police Superintendent Blake loaned us cots. Kids signed up and we gathered some older Y members as staff. We hired a local cook. The food was great.

We played football, told stories, swam, and had outdoor campfires and sing-alongs. The music was amazing.

Each night we gathered the staff together to reflect on the day and plan the next day's activities. One of the staff suggested that it would build group spirit if each night we each had one glass of rum punch. This was way outside my frame of understanding, but I thought, *Let's get with the programme.* So staff development always ended with a glass of rum punch.

Two summers later, we had another camp, in Balandra near Toco.

We decided to add six kids from the Boys Industrial School in Diego Martin.

These were tough kids. I met with them before the camp to suggest that this was a chance for them to be part of a very wonderful experience but — and this was big — they needed to behave.

The first day, one of our staff had their wallet stolen while they were in the ocean swimming. Big problem. I went to what I took to be the leader of the group. I said this could be serious and if one of the kids from the Boys Industrial School had taken the wallet, then they would all have to leave. He said, "Give me thirty minutes." I did.

He came back and told me none of the kids from the school had taken the wallet. I asked how he could be so sure. He told me I wouldn't want to know. He asked for another two hours and he would have the wallet returned to the staff member. He was as good to his word. The wallet came back and there was no more stealing during the camp.

We borrowed a movie projector from the Canadian High Commission and, twice a week, we would get two large white sheets and have outdoor movies. The whole village (some 300 people) would show up.

The tradition of a glass of rum punch for the staff each evening continued.

Looking back, we made do with little, but for our kids, it was a special time that they would not soon forget. For me too!

President and champs

A TEN-DAY summer camp for boys, drawn from various parts of the country, culminated last night with a dinner and a camp fire at the Carenage Girls' Government School.

Under Camp Wardens Gordon Cressy and Eric Bojesen, loaned by the National Council of YMCA's of Canada, the 42 youths taking part did a little of every thing.

Of the four groups in the camp, the Best Boy award went to Anthony Lake, who was also named the outstanding camper.

● PICTURE shows YMCA President Dennis Mahabir admiring a plaque won by the winning group — Silver Stars. At left is Camp Warden Cressy.

"Evening News,"

Govt. ought to do more for youths says leader

A CANADIAN youth leader believes that the Trinidad Government should do a lot more for the young people of the country.

"More and more attention should be paid to the needs of the young people as the future of the nation depends on the youths," said Mr. Gordon Cressy, 21, now in Trinidad to run a youth camp at Carenage.

The camp for boys between 10 and 13 years of age is being sponsored and financed by the YMCA of Port-of-Spain.

Mr. Cressy will be assisted in the running of the camp by another Canadian, Mr. Eric Robinson.

Agenda

Mr. Cressy pointed out that at camp the boys will be "ready to do everything sparked of men living in the outdoors."

Under the guidance and instruction of Mr. Cressy and Mr. Robinson, both being acting instructors, the boys will also be taught "how to get along with other people. This is much better than dealing in fractions and figures," said Mr. Cressy.

The Chicago Stories 1964–1967

In the fall of 1964, I said goodbye to my parents again and headed off to George Williams College on the south side of Chicago. It was a fascinating time. Martin Luther King and Jesse Jackson had moved north to Chicago to expose institutional racism. I went one night to listen to Martin Luther King speak at a church on the south side of Chicago. The place was packed. There were only a few white people in attendance. Clearly some of the Black attendees were opposed to Dr. King. At the time, many were embracing the Black Muslim movement, headquartered on the south side of Chicago, led by Elijah Muhammed and Malcolm X (though later they had a falling out).

Dr. King started speaking, and immediately, a small group of people tried to shout him down. I watched, fascinated, as Dr. King stopped for a moment and, in a calm voice, said, "Obviously, some of our Black brothers do not agree with my position here, and I would invite one of them to come to the podium to make their case." One person did come up and spoke for several minutes.

Dr. King came back and suggested that, since those angry voices had made their case, they should be respectful of his voice. There was quiet in the room. Then Dr. King took flight and, in a soaring voice, made the strong case for racial equality. It was riveting. The standing ovation went on and on, and I went back to my dorm the wiser for having been there.

A few days later, Jesse Jackson came to our college, and a small group of us went to listen. As I recall, I was the only white person in the group. Jackson talked about the need for community organizing at the grassroots level to effect permanent change. He made a lot of sense. When it came time for questions, I suggested that sometimes for this to happen we need to experience things in different places. I said that my time spent in Trinidad had helped me to see beyond my experience of growing up in white middle-class North Toronto.

He looked at the group, then me, and said, "That is fine for you, but for us, we grow up in the community and that is where our organizing begins." A useful lesson that.

Learn by Doing: Get Out in the Community

As part of my college education, I had to do two fieldwork placements.

One of my placements was at the Division Street YMCA and the other was at the Elliott Donnelley Youth Center at 3947 South Michigan on the south side of Chicago.

Division Street YMCA

The Division St. Y served people from many different backgrounds, including Puerto Rican, African American, and Polish. Virtually everyone was low income.

In addition to my student placement, I supported myself by teaching swimming at the Y, three nights a week and all day Saturday. Some of our kids were very good swimmers, and one of them suggested we start a swim team. The Y had never had a swim team, and I had only barely made my high school swim team. But, always the keener, I decided to give it a try. We got a stopwatch, had a couple of tryouts, began practising, got faster, and had some fun.

We entered the city championships and, amazingly, finished in the top eight in a few events. This qualified us to participate in the state championship. We packed into the Y van and headed to Peoria for the state finals. In truth, we did not do very well. But we did get excited when our relay team finished strong and snagged eighth spot. We all cheered — you would have thought we won the gold medal! We drove back to the Y tired but happy.

I suggested we have a celebratory potluck dinner. As a kid, I remember going to father-and-son banquets. One of the kids told me we would have a better turnout with a mother-and-son banquet — and he was right. So we invited everyone — moms, dads, grandparents, brothers, and sisters. Getting to the state final was a huge reason to celebrate.

Elliott Donnelley Youth Center, Brownsville, South Side Chicago

When I first went to the Elliott Donnelley Youth Center, I told the executive director, Mr. Gleason, that I wanted to do something significant in my placement. It turned out I was the only white person at the centre as either kid or staff. I told him of my experience in Trinidad, of hearing Martin Luther King speak, and of my commitment to working hard to make things happen. He listened patiently and said, "Gordon, we are pleased to have you here. Your resume indicates you are a very good swim instructor and you play a good game of table tennis, and we do need a good swim instructor." I pressed on, stressing that I believed I could really make a difference doing something important. He smiled and said, "Well, Gordon, we do have a problem in the neighbourhood with venereal disease, and I would like you to wipe it out."

I went back to my dorm that night and thought about it. I remembered that, back in high school at Lawrence Park Collegiate, we watched movies on family-life studies. It struck me that, if we could show one of these films to the young people, they might get the message. I called the Toronto Board of Education. They told me they had such a film, called *Dance Little Children*, and they would send it down.

I mention now that, years later, when I became a school trustee and eventually chair of the Toronto Board of Education, that film was removed from the curriculum — and rightly so!

One evening I brought about eighteen young people together to watch the film. In it, there's a dance attended by lots of teenagers. One couple leaves early and goes off to the boy's house. The parents are not home. There's lots of footage of the house, and eventually the couple goes into the bedroom. Being filmed a long time ago, the camera does not follow — but we knew what was going on. To cut the story short, the young woman discovers a rash, which she thinks is measles, and goes to the doctor. The doctor diagnoses the problem as venereal disease and indicates that, if he could get the different contacts this young woman's boyfriend had, he could start to deal with the problem. The movie fades out on the dance.

I turned to the young people and said, "Did you get the message?"

One tall guy at the back stood up with a smile on his face and said, "Yes, sir. The white kids can't dance!"

Everyone laughed except me. It took a while, but I did get it. They were right. It was a white movie for a white audience, and on top of that, the kids did not dance very well at all.

Lesson learned: Start where people are to solve a problem.

Good thing the youth centre still needed a swim instructor. Soon I was back in the pool teaching swimming.

That movie is still available on YouTube. Search for "Dance, Little Children (Kansas State Board of Health, 1965)." It has not aged well.

"Our People Have Been Waiting Their Whole Lives"

It was a tough time on the south side of Chicago in 1967. The Blackstone Rangers gang, under the charismatic leadership of Jeff Fort, was expanding across the city. A year later, race riots broke out after the assassination of Martin Luther King.

Our kids were not immune to the attraction of this gang. We pressed ahead with activities at the youth centre to give the kids alternative experiences. Many of the kids' moms got involved too. One of them suggested the kids go on a trip as a grand adventure. She thought Niagara Falls would be a good place to go. Soon the plan took shape.

We would take the centre van, pile ten kids into it (this was long before we worried about insurance, seat belts, or numbers), and drive to Niagara Falls and then on to Toronto. We would stay at the downtown Toronto YMCA, visit City Hall, and have a barbeque dinner with my parents.

We needed to raise some money for the trip. The mothers hosted a fried chicken lunch, which was terrific, but we still needed to raise more money. One of the moms suggested I meet with the local alderman, Ralph Metcalfe, to see if he would help. This became my introduction to politics — and my introduction to becoming a politician myself. She suggested I go early to his Tuesday-night constituency hours, which started at 7:00 p.m. So off I went to meet Alderman Ralph Metcalfe at 7:00 p.m. sharp.

Now Ralph Metcalfe was no ordinary alderman. In his youth, he was an outstanding sprinter who won two silver medals in the 100-metre race at the 1932 and 1936 Olympic Games. He was part of the Richard Daley Democratic machine, which dominated Chicago politics for years.

I was the third person to arrive but other people were allowed in before me. This went on and on. First, I was frustrated, then angry. Finally, when no one was left, I went in. He smiled and asked how I was doing. I could not hold back and told him I was angry having to wait that long. He looked up, and I will never forget what he said: "I understand, but you need to understand our people have been waiting their whole lives — now what can I do for you?"

I told him our plan. He liked it and wrote out a cheque for $100 on the spot. He then asked where the kids lived. I told him they all lived at 4120 South Prairie, a high-rise building nearby. (This building was torn down some years ago, but there is a neat video of it and the people who lived there on YouTube.)

Then Alderman Metcalfe did an amazing thing — he went through his card file and told me to bring the moms to meet with Mr. Green, who lived in an apartment in that building, and he would give us $50. We went to Mr. Green's apartment. The moms told the story and he gave us the money. Mr. Green was known in the building as the precinct captain. He worked for Alderman Metcalfe, and his job was to make good things happen in the building.

Alderman Metcalfe kept getting elected, eventually serving three terms in Congress. From him I learned to keep close to the street, a powerful lesson in grassroot politics.

So off we went from Chicago, touring Niagara Falls en route to Toronto.

The kids stayed at the old Toronto YMCA residence on College Street. We met Bill Dennison, who was mayor of Toronto at the time. We all went to my parents' house for a backyard barbeque dinner. This was 1967 and I was certain most people on our street had never met a Black person. Our kids had never seen a street like ours or, for that matter, seen a group of white people living in a neighbourhood. As the van pulled up outside our house, the neighbours stared. Our kids did too.

Then my dad came off the porch and said in a booming voice, "Welcome." He broke the ice. We went in the backyard to eat. My parents had invited some of the neighbours. It was uncomfortable at first.

We found a topic we all could share: baseball. Our neighbours all knew about Fergie Jenkins, the new pitcher for the Chicago Cubs who was Canadian and hailed from Chatham. The kids knew their team, the Chicago Cubs well, so we talked about baseball and had steak and potato chips.

At the end of the evening, we all shook hands. The kids were not into hugging. A couple of them exchanged addresses with a couple of the neighbours' kids. It would be nice to say that they became lifelong pen pals, but it did not happen.

After overnighting at the Y residence, we headed back down the QEW to Detroit and on to Chicago. It was an excellent adventure.

I kept in touch with the kids for a couple of years. I heard one of them had been shot to death. I sometimes wonder where they are today and how they are doing. I decided to try and find out. After some digging on Facebook, I found Mr. Arnold Coleman, who lived at 4120 Prairie for many years and knew these kids growing up. We talked at length. He shared with me that despite the problems in 4120 Prairie, there was a sense of community and of family. He got tired of going to funerals and started an annual 4120 Prairie Cruise to celebrate the best parts of that community.

The sad reality though is that only a few of the kids I worked and played with back in 1967 are alive today. I tracked down one of the kids, Nate McMorris, now living in a seniors' residence in Minneapolis. He remembers the trip to Toronto vividly and talked about meeting my parents. It was an emotional conversation for both of us.

About twenty-five years ago, while in Chicago for a U of T alumni event, I went back to visit the Elliott Donnelley Youth Center. The staff person asked what I was doing there. I told him I used to work there. He was surprised to see a white person. He noticed that I had driven there and suggested that I should leave. He said, not in a mean way, that it just was not safe to be in the area.

A few years ago, I called to see how things were going some fifty years after I had worked there. The truth is that they are no better. The youth centre, though, remains a safe haven for kids and a place where real opportunity exists for them to learn and grow.

Race Riots

The major race riot in Chicago occurred after Martin Luther King was assassinated in 1968. But I experienced two riots while in Chicago. The first was in the spring of 1966, when the members of the Puerto Rican community demonstrated loudly for three nights on Division Street, near the YMCA where I worked. I watched from the street corner as police confronted the largely male crowd. Actually, it was pretty scary. Many women were banging pots and pans from their second-floor windows and encouraging the demonstrators below. The police with their blowhorns were telling the women to stop. I clearly remember a humorous moment when a couple of the women shouted back, "We do not speak English!" The banging carried on.

In May of 1967, long-simmering tensions between residents and the police on the south side of Chicago broke out. Staff at the youth centre told me to leave. They said, we know you and like you, but in a race riot you are on the wrong side. I was profoundly affected by this as I felt the youth centre was where I belonged. Being white, I was the wrong person, in the wrong place, at the wrong time.

"Go Home and See If You Can Make a Difference There."

I was graduating in the spring of 1967. I had been accepted to graduate school at the University of Chicago and hired on as a dorm advisor, so my accommodation cost was covered. I went back to Mr. Gleason at the Elliott Donnelley Youth Center and told him of my plans. I wanted to live my life out on the south side of Chicago and make a real difference in the world of race relations. He listened patiently, as he had done before. Then he looked me in the eye and said, "Gordon, you are a good guy, but frankly you are not going to make much of a difference here. Go home and see if you can make a difference there."

I was completely devastated. I stayed in my room staring at the wall for two days. Then, reluctantly, I accepted that he was right, and packed up and came home to Toronto.

Reflections on My Experiences in Trinidad and Chicago

Looking back, the experiences in these two settings changed the direction of my life forever. I had been heading for a career in business, following in my father's footsteps. What I came to realize was that making money was not a driving force for me anymore.

I had seen up close the unfairness in society. It seemed to me that trying to even the odds, especially in terms of race, was a worthwhile life goal.

In many ways it was my introduction to examining white privilege, but I certainly had no idea about that back then. I headed back to Toronto to take my master of social work at the University of Toronto.

Back to School and Work in Toronto

I enrolled in the School of Social Work at the University of Toronto and moved in with two terrific roommates, Wally Seccombe and Peter Turner. We found an apartment above Stanley's Variety Store on Ontario Street near Regent Park, a very large public housing project. Our landlord, Al Sisberg, was a Polish Jew who'd been on the run from the Germans during the Second World War. He had often slept in the fields during the cold of winter. Unfortunately for us, his ground-floor store controlled the heat for the whole building. I remember coming to him one very cold January day to complain that our apartment was really cold. "Cold," he said. "You have no idea what cold is!"

In early September, I learned that the Atkinson Foundation had given a $5,000 grant to the YMCA to develop a pilot After-4 programme at Rose Avenue Public School in the heart of the newly developed St. James Town. The idea was that many kids had no parent at home after school, and the school facilities could provide useful activities for these students. I remember going to the interview on a Wednesday afternoon and being asked, "When could the programme start?" I gathered they wanted a quick start, so I blurted out we would be ready to go on Monday. They liked the answer and called me that night to offer me the job. And, yes, we did open on the Monday! I called some new friends from the School of Social Work, got in touch with some old friends, and soon we had a neat group of volunteers leading a variety of activities: floor hockey, dodge ball, cooking, and visits to nearby historic sights. Amazingly, the programme took off — more kids signed up, more activities were added. The principal, Miss Warren, was pleased; the kids and their parents liked what was going on; and the YMCA soon developed an After-4 programme that went across the city. Years later, the RBC Foundation took this model and provided funding to schools across the country.

Central Neighbourhood House

In 1968, my fieldwork placement at the U of T School of Social Work was at the settlement house, Central Neighbourhood House, then located on Sherbourne Street. This was only a five-minute walk from my apartment on Ontario Street. I worked with a group of twelve-year-old boys, organizing group activities.

In early 1969, Central Neighbourhood announced they were moving to a location on Ontario Street to be nearer to Regent Park. The more important reason for the move was that the property on Ontario Street was much cheaper to purchase.

The neighbours were not happy with the idea of a settlement house moving onto a residential street. A young John Sewell organized a meeting to protest this move. As a neighbour, I attended the meeting to support my neighbours in opposition to the move. The next day, my social work supervisor called me in to say she was not happy with my attendance at the meeting. She asked if I planned to graduate. She told me that, as a field-placement student, I was expected to be loyal to Central Neighbourhood House, not out demonstrating with the neighbours. And that was that.

I failed my fieldwork placement and had to appeal to the dean in order to graduate.

John Sewell was elected as an alderman later that fall, and Central Neighbourhood House did move onto Ontario Street.

Opportunity House — The Group Home

While I was at school, from time to time I would be asked to speak about my experiences in Trinidad and Chicago. I enjoyed public speaking, still do, and became quite good at it.

One day I was talking to group of men at the Armour Heights Rotary Club.

At the end of the talk, two of the members, Andy Hazlett and Harry Trotter, came up and asked what my plans were after graduation. At that point, I had no idea. I had married Marsha Endahl that past August and knew I needed to get a decent job. They talked to me about Opportunity House, a group home in the east end for teenage boys who had been in trouble with the law. Apparently, the home had struggled in the neighbourhood and was currently closed. One thing I have learned over the years is this: People like group homes. The farther they are located from where they live the more they like them.

Andy and Harry proposed that my wife and I move in, reopen the home, and bring in eight teenage boys, aged fourteen to seventeen, to live in the home as an alternative to training school. I was intrigued by the idea, excited about free room and board, and, after chatting with Marsha, we accepted the challenge.

Each of the boys had a story. Some came from difficult home settings, some had hooked up with the wrong friends, all had been in trouble with the law.

Two have stayed in my mind all these years. Kevin Ackroyd was the stepson of Deputy Chief of Police Jack Ackroyd (he became the chief a few years later). Kevin was a particularly bright kid and often frustrated the math teacher at Riverdale Collegiate when he came up with the answer before the teacher did.

Vince Benedictus came from a large close-knit Italian family. He and Kevin became buddies, and they came to us with the idea that the group should travel out west in the summer. Having seen the success of the Chicago kids coming to Toronto, I jumped at the idea — but with conditions.

The kids' marks had to be okay and they would have to raise some money.

They agreed and started to sell sand candles to neighbours and family friends.

The folks at Corrections Canada agreed to provide seed money if we documented the trip. In early July 1969, we took off, heading first to Ottawa (no one had been to the capital before), then to Montreal, and then made the trek out west in a rented van. We hired my friends Peter Turner and Jimmie Wolfe to take charge of this adventure.

They hiked, swam, slept in tents, and went mountain climbing, successfully climbing Table Mountain. In Vancouver, they attended a rock concert and then spent a couple of days on Wreck Beach near Vancouver, where they met a young woman in her twenties who they enjoyed talking to. She said her name was Margaret Sinclair and she was going to marry Pierre Trudeau. The boys thought this was the funniest thing … until a few months later when she and Pierre did get married!

The federal government staff came to interview the boys, hoping that they would talk about leadership, team building, the joy of hiking, and the great outdoors. The boys were excited about the trip but said the highlight for them was the rock concert in Vancouver!

I often wondered if there was any real impact from this trip. Several years ago, I got a call out of the blue from Vince Benedictus's wife. She was having a surprise sixtieth birthday party for Vince and wondered if we could attend. She said Vince often talked positively about his time at Opportunity House and that his trip out west was the highlight. My wife, Joanne, and I went. I had not seen Vince in over forty years, but we recognized each other instantly, and both cried and laughed at the same time.

These moments affirm why we do what we do.

Education Stories

Chair, Toronto Board of Education, 1975 and 1976.

My work in Chicago and at Opportunity House was challenging and exciting … but it was not enough. I was spending my time helping kids adapt to the system. I came to realize that part of the problem was the system itself.

In 1969, I ran for office for the first time and was elected school trustee with the Toronto Board of Education. (More on this election campaign later.) My seven years spent in education politics (two years as chair of the board), were among the most exciting and rewarding of my career.

What follows is a series of stories about how we worked to change the face of education in Toronto. I end this section with two personal experiences about teachers and the education system.

Banning the Strap and the Legacy of Vern Copeland

In 1971, the Toronto Board of Education became the first school system in Canada to ban corporal punishment — that is, the strap. A group of progressive trustees, led by Fiona Nelson, pushed this through over the objections of the Principals' Council and the Teachers' Federations and some vocal parents. As a young school trustee, I joined the group. I must admit that, during the debate, I naively tried an amendment that would allow local schools to make their own decision, a throwback to the argument for community control of the schools. Fortunately for me, that amendment was ruled out of order.

Other school jurisdictions continued to shy away from the issue, but the decision to ban the strap continued to simmer for the next few years as discipline in the schools remained a problem.

In late 1974, word spread that the Elementary Teachers' Federation, the Principals' Association, and some parent groups were organizing to "bring back the strap." At this point, no other jurisdiction had joined the Toronto Board's lead.

I had just been elected chair of the board to take office at the start of 1975, and it looked like this was to be my first major issue. As I counted votes, I realized that a motion to reintroduce the strap was going to win. I felt deeply about this issue and was pondering different approaches. Frankly, though, there seemed no way out — the votes seemed locked and the board meeting was approaching quickly. Still,

I was organizing as best I could with my close trustee friends Doug Barr and Dan Leckie. One trustee, Vern Copeland, a supporter of our position, was nowhere to be found. Vern was a second-term trustee and, at twenty-six, one of the youngest. He taught psychology at York University. I left messages but got no call back — this, of course, was long before cellphones and emails.

On the Monday before the board meeting, I got a call from Vern. He was in hospital. He told me he had terminal cancer and the doctors had told him he had not long to live. While I was trying to absorb this shocking news, Vern said he wanted to come and speak at the board meeting on Thursday evening and oppose the reintroduction of the strap. Of course, I said yes.

On Thursday evening, there was a massive turnout. In addition to the public space, the meeting was broadcast live in another room.

Vern Copeland arrived in a business suit and was clearly very unwell — he looked grey. This item was first up on the agenda, and I acknowledged Vern as the first speaker.

Vern, in a clear but quiet voice, started off: "Ladies and gentlemen, this is the last time any of you will see me alive. I rise to speak today to oppose in the strongest possible terms the reintroduction of the strap in our school system." The room went quiet. Vern then spoke straight from the heart, making a persuasive argument to retain the strap ban. When Vern sat down, there was a hush in the room, then strong applause from those quarters wanting to retain the ban on the strap.

Those seeking to bring the strap back knew it was over. And it was. Vern went back to his hospital bed, and that Sunday he passed away.

On the Monday, at his funeral, I told Vern's parents the extraordinary impact of his remarks. The strap never came back and, over the years, other jurisdictions across Canada joined the Toronto Board in banning the strap.

I am usually a strong believer in "no surprises" but in this instance Vern's presence alone stopped the reintroduction of the strap in its tracks.

For Vern Copeland, a fitting legacy indeed.

Frankland Public School and John Restakis

In the early 1970s, parents across the school system were seeking more involvement in the schools. Community involvement and community schools became the rallying cry. The traditional Home and School Association was being replaced by school community councils that had a much higher degree of influence and involvement in the operation of the school.

This change was either embraced or resisted. A key to making this work was the local principal. Frankland Public School, built in 1910 on Logan Ave in the east end of the city, had a great principal in Cecil Martindale. He was smart, jovial, and had a reputation for getting things done. He got the school community council going.

This group identified the need for a wholesale renovation of the school and the playground.

At the same time, John Restakis was a young school community relations worker. John had trained as a community organizer and his job was focused on the integration of school and community. He was part of a fledgling new department at the Toronto Board. John, having Greek heritage, was assigned to Frankland because of the large number of people of Greek origin surrounding the school.

One cold winter evening, I arrived at the school a little early to help set up for the school community council meeting. Usually about twelve people attended. I bumped into John Restakis in the hallway and inquired why he was there as he had never attended a school community council meeting. He told me he was having a meeting with parents to talk about teaching the Greek language in the school as a regular part of the school programme. This heritage-language approach was being discussed in many schools at that time. I asked how many parents he expected to attend. He floored me completely when he said about eighty.

There were two meetings happening simultaneously on different floors — one in English and one in Greek. John, ever the bold strategist, suggested to me that at some point in the meeting there would be merit in the two groups talking together. He was right and we did. Each group supported the other, and a new school community council was born. For the first couple of years the meetings were conducted in both English and Greek. And yes, the school got its major renovation and the Greek Heritage Language programme started at Frankland Public School, proving once again that, when people join forces around a common cause, good things can and do happen.

John Restakis went on to a distinguished career in the cooperative economic field around the globe. The current website at Frankland Public School notes: "At Frankland we honour the partnership between school, home and community." To be frank, I have no idea if there is a direct line from that powerful statement and the origins of the school community council back in the mid-1970s. What I do know for sure is, on that cold February night, something quite spectacular occurred.

Parkway Vocational School and Fitz Blackman

Fitz Blackman came from Trinidad. His father had been the mayor of Port of Spain. He was a young and very good music teacher. He was also very funny. Unfortunately, it was a hard time to find work in the school system. He could not get a job at a collegiate or a technical school, but he found a job at Parkway Vocational School (which no longer exists). The vocational schools were designed for students of limited academic ability and were all located south of Bloor Street.

After a couple of months, Fitz went to the school principal and said he wanted to start a school band. The principal told him they had never had a band as it was unlikely to succeed with these kids, but that the goal was to get the kids to sing. Fitz was undeterred. He went down to see Harvey Perrin, the head of music at the Toronto Board of Education. Harvey was impressed, while a little skeptical. A pilot project was proposed and, a few months later, the Parkway School Band was preforming at the Kiwanis Music Festival!

They did not win a prize, but they were darn good. Music educators came to ask him how he had accomplished this. Fitz just smiled and said, "In my home country, we invented the steel band after the Second World War. Most of the original people who played the pan came from the streets of Laventille Hill [a poor area on the outskirts of Port of Spain]. I believed in these kids and they came through." As a matter of fact, a number of years later the steel band was introduced into Toronto schools and has become very popular.

A couple of months later, the head of the guidance department came to Fitz and asked if he had any ideas about what to do with a few of the kids who were loud, acting out, and disrupting the class. Fitz said, "Send them down to me." That happened. Most of the kids returned to the class an hour later calm and ready to engage in classwork. The social worker thought this was a small miracle and wondered what amazing new therapy programme Fitz Blackman knew about that worked with these kids. Fitz just said, "I had them blow the French Horn for forty-five minutes … that usually works." Sometimes simple works.

The Secondary School Teachers' Strike, November 12, 1975 – January 12, 1976

"Catch Up and Keep Up" — The Teachers' Rallying Cry

In 1975, interest rates were going through the roof and inflation was high. Teachers in other parts of the province were getting significant salary increases.

The right to strike had recently been implemented by Ontario Premier Bill Davis and Minister of Education Tom Wells.

Teacher expectations in the Toronto area were high. The Elementary Teachers' Federation had a tentative agreement with the school boards that was, wait for it, a 12 percent increase in the first year and 10 percent in the second year!! We are talking about a different time zone for sure.

The secondary teachers thought they could do better and advised their elementary colleagues to hold off signing the collective agreement.

The negotiations dragged through the summer months and into the fall, with a fact-finding report by well-known heavyweight lawyer Stanley Hartt. The Ontario Secondary School Teachers' Federation and the boards of education were represented by two highly regarded lawyers, Aubrey Golden and Dick Shibley.

In early October, there were rumblings that the Government of Canada was considering a major policy initiative to deal with escalating wages and costs.

As chair of the Toronto Board of Education, I was invited to Ottawa to talk with Donald Macdonald, the minister of finance and my member of Parliament. I briefed him on the state of negotiations and told him it was looking bleak. He asked me if we could settle by Thanksgiving Monday night. It being Friday, I said that would be difficult. He said he could not tell me what was about to happen, but he strongly advised that we try and settle.

I flew back to Toronto and briefed our negotiating team. Being the holiday weekend, there were no negotiations scheduled. We were unable to reach Stanley Hartt — so no negotiations happened.

On Monday night, October 13, 1975, Prime Minister Pierre Trudeau went on national television to announce a new wage and price controls policy of 6 percent in the first year and 4 percent in the second year. He further said that any contracts signed that night before midnight would be exempt from the new policy. The Elementary Teachers' Federation called to say, let us seal the deal and sign off. Two days later, the elementary teachers voted overwhelmingly in favour of the agreement.

The Secondary Teachers' Federation, though, were ready to strike. The excitement at a rally at Maple Leaf Gardens was overwhelming. The teachers voted over 90 percent in favour of the strike. The boards of education in Toronto, emboldened by the prime minister's position on wage and price controls, dug in their heels.

On November 12, 1975, the strike was on. It would be the first legal major teacher strike in Ontario's history.

There were 8,800 teachers out on the picket line for the first time. Only 50 teachers crossed the line. In those days, principals and vice principals were part of the teachers' federations but had to be in school. Most donated their salaries to the federation and many brought coffee out for the teachers on the line.

The early days for the teachers were euphoric, cathartic, and exciting. The teachers believed they were going to win and be back in the classroom in a few days.

This all changed when the school board officials went to Ottawa to meet with the newly created Anti-Inflation Board (AIB). This board, chaired by Federal Cabinet Minister Jean-Luc Pépin, had been set up to give guidance to ongoing collective bargaining discussions. The AIB ruled that the Board of Education's offer to the teachers was too high!

This was a game changer. Things went from fun and excitement to bitterness and hostility very fast. The media generally supported the boards over the teachers. Parents would call in and say, "Get back to the bargaining table and reduce the offer!"

The negotiations moved to the Royal York Hotel. Meanwhile the teachers were outside on the picket line, and it was getting colder.

At a personal level, this was all overwhelming. I had been in many protest marches and had been part of picket lines before. This time, though, as chair of the board, I was management and crossing the picket line, and it was uncomfortable — but it was my job. So I did it.

Some of my high school buddies, Gary McNeil, Bill Furse, and David Wells, were teachers. They were feeling that no one was saying good things about them. They suggested I put out a statement. I worked with Michael Cobden, formerly a reporter with the *Toronto Star* and now in charge of communications at the Toronto Board of Education.

I hosted a press conference and made two points. One, that we had a serious salary difference to resolve. But two, after the strike was over, our teachers, who were good people, would be back in the classroom with our students.

Most teachers were grateful, as they saw this as affirming who they were.

Some members of the teachers' negotiating team were not happy, as it changed the channel from me being the enemy.

As we closed in on Christmas, there was a mood to try and resolve this. Clearly some on both sides wanted to settle and others did not. There was a lot of drinking going on at the hotel. One evening Bill Ross, chair of the Metropolitan Toronto School Board, and Doug Dinsmore, the head of the teachers' negotiating team, went out to dinner with the intention of coming up with a deal.

We waited up. Finally, Bill Ross came into the room, a little drunk, and announced with real flair that he and Doug had a deal. When we asked about the details, he pulled out a serviette with writing on it. But — and here is where it went south — Bill could not read what had been written! I gather the same went for Doug Dinsmore. Sadly, we went off for the holiday season with no deal — nor, for that matter, was there a deal in sight.

Teachers were becoming increasingly concerned. Some of them were taking part-time jobs at the post office to get through the holiday period.

The first week of January came and went with no progress. The Education Relations Commission had been set up to advise the government when a strike was going to affect the students' school year. This group was now in play.

We learned that some in the teacher leadership were concerned that teachers had had enough and were talking about going back to class. A principle of strikes has always been solidarity … we go out together and we go back in together. The government introduced back-to-work legislation and, though the Secondary School Teachers' Federation officially opposed it, they clearly wanted it to pass. Jim Foulds the NDP education critic led the NDP opposition to the legislation (but not too loudly and not for too long).

On January 12, 1976, the strike ended two months after it had begun. The final settlement that the province, the federal government, and the school boards approved was basically the same as the original offer.

When classes resumed, it was not an easy time. Lingering anger was evident. Many teachers in the technical schools, who had been members of other unions that had experienced strikes, had been through this before and found their stride more easily. For others, though, it really was the end of innocence.

For me, it was extremely difficult. I had been viewed as a friend of labour unions. I was used to being "the good guy." But friendships were strained. There was no joy in any of this.

A couple of months later, one of my principal friends, Bob Beardsley, invited me to visit his school, Eastdale Collegiate, to meet with the teachers. He thought the time was ripe. Apparently not. I arrived and went to the staff room. One by one the teachers got up and left without acknowledging me. Finally, John Brown, a teacher I knew well, was the last to get up. He came over, put an arm around my shoulder, and said, "Gord, don't take it personally."

But, of course, I did.

Streaming Kids to Vocational School — Marilyn Miller and Joy Tepperman

At the beginning of the 1970s, there was a strong perception that immigrant kids were being "streamed" into the bottom level vocational schools. Anecdotal evidence was mounting, and the media was starting to take notice. But there was no hard evidence.

Enter Marilyn Miller, a social worker at the Toronto Board of Education.

She was witnessing this firsthand every day. She was joined by Joy Tepperman, a contract employee hired to assist Marilyn on a government-funded Local Initiatives Project grant.

Joy was an aspiring writer and quickly saw the need to document the problem.

Over several months, they prepared a well-researched and documented report showing that systemic streaming of immigrant kids was going on. They submitted their report to John Boys, the head of the social work department. He said he would get back to them as to next steps. Then they waited. And waited. Nothing happened. No response at all.

Finally, in frustration, they came and met with me, an elected official. They knew they were doing an end run on the system — but they wanted action.

For me, this was like mana from heaven. A bombshell report exposing the system. I quickly organized a major press conference. The media all turned out. The story was told and all hell broke loose. There was a fair bit of "how dare they tell this story to the public" since the "system" was still working on its response to the report. Joy and Marilyn were threatened with a legal suit.

The trustees, however, had gotten the information they needed to dig deeper, and a Vocational Schools Task Force was set up under the leadership of a fantastic educator, Donald Rutledge, who was determined to see this through. And that was the beginning of the end of the vocational schools and systemic streaming.

For Marilyn and Joy, this threat of a legal suit was disconcerting. Marilyn asked if I knew a lawyer. I called my friend Warren Seyffert and he agreed to meet with them. Warren was a very fine lawyer and, from what I could see, he operated in the Robin Hood tradition of charging his wealthy clients a lot and often not charging others at all.

We went in to meet with Warren and he listened patiently. He said that he could defend them if it came to that. He then asked if they had any money. Marilyn said she was a young social worker and had a little. Joy, a contract worker, also had very little, but then she said something very intriguing, "I am a writer and someday I am going to write books and be very successful."

In the end, the legal suit never went forward. Joy Tepperman took the writing name of Joy Fielding and has now written over twenty-five published books and is viewed as one of Canada's most successful writers. Oh, and she married Warren Seyffert! Sometimes serendipity works!

One more thing … several years back, I was meeting with Joan Randall, who was chair of the governing council of U of T. Somehow, we wound up chatting about Warren Seyffert. They were both on the board of the Royal Ontario Museum. I told her how Warren and I had worked together over many years on various community projects. I told her how I valued his Robin Hood approach to the law ... charging his wealthy clients a lot and then taking on some disadvantaged clients for free. What I did not know was that Warren was her lawyer. She changed lawyers shortly after our conversation. Warren was not happy with me. Fortunately, we laugh about this incident today.

Teaching

When I was a school trustee, my salary for the first three years was only $3,600. It later took what I viewed as a huge bump up to $6,000. I was looking to supplement my income and thought that I might be a good fit at the Ontario Institute for Studies in Education, teaching in the sociology department. I applied and, because of my grassroots experience, was accepted to teach a couple of courses: Community and the School, and the Politics of Urban Education. The challenge was to bring the theory behind these real experiences to the table.

I got excited by this opportunity and found myself teaching primarily full-time teachers who were doing their masters of education part time, mainly in the evening. For my first class, I prepared well and delivered what I thought was a well-researched and balanced lecture. To my dismay, I noticed three or four of the students nod off. At break time, I asked a couple of the students for feedback. They both said that while the lecture was interesting it was not entertaining. These teachers had taught all day, had rushed down to the Ontario Institute for Studies in Education (OISE) on Bloor Street to make the class, and frankly they were tired. I got the message.

Over the next few years, I developed into a good storyteller, and I also invited guests who were in the middle of the action to speak to the students. What was most amazing was that, during the teachers' strike, our classes went on. So teachers who were on strike continued to come to class, and I brought in representatives from the Secondary

School Teachers' Federation and the school boards. One class member suggested to both parties that, rather than negotiating at the Royal York Hotel, if they would meet outside in the cold, like the teachers were, getting a settlement would come quite quickly! This was met with applause.

I enjoyed teaching, and the teachers helped me learn and reflect.

After ten years, I had left my political role in education and moved on to Toronto City Council, and it was time to leave OISE.

A decade later, when I was a vice president of the University of Toronto, I was asked by my colleagues whether I would like to teach a course in the Faculty of Social Work. This seemed like a good way to keep connected to the university community. I had a great run and followed my learnings at OISE by telling some good stories and bringing in some terrific community activists to share their experiences.

My old professor at the School of Social Work, Dr. Ben Shapiro, was retiring. The dean of Social Work, Heather Munro-Blume, asked me to attend his farewell party at her house and make a few remarks. I agreed and went back and found my graduate thesis that I had written for him. It was about Regent Park. I learned through interviews that, when people needed advice or help, rather than go to a social worker, psychologist, or psychiatrist, people went to the shopkeeper, the bartender, and each other. I had written a series of stories detailing these experiences. He gave me a B– and wrote something like, "Gordon, you write great stories, but the paper is lacking in theoretical analysis."

The afternoon of Ben's retirement event, I had my end-of-term class with my Social Work students. By this time, students were evaluating professors. The class went well and the students left. I sat back and read the mostly positive assessments. Then one comment leapt out at me ... it was like the ghost of Ben Shapiro past! The student wrote, "You tell good stories, but the course is lacking in intellectual rigour or theoretical analysis."

And that is how my teaching career ended. I did go to Ben Shapiro's farewell, and I told the story of how it was clear, based on these two experiences over twenty years apart, that I had not changed a bit!

Be Proactive and Reach Out

My son Keith was in Grade 1 at Brown Public School. On the Friday of the first week, we got a note to say the teacher was being replaced by a supply teacher.

Two weeks later, we got a similar note. This was upsetting to us and other parents, as stability and consistency in the classroom are important, particularly in the early years.

Parents started to call each other. A few parents, knowing of my background as a school trustee, got in touch with me, and we agreed that we should have a meeting with the principal to discuss our concern. The meeting was set up for the coming Monday.

Imagine then our shock and dismay when that Friday we got another note about a new teacher. On Sunday, I was at home when I got a call from this new teacher. She told me she was starting on Monday and that she hoped to be there for the rest of the year.

I told her how upset we parents were about the revolving door of teachers in the classroom. She said she understood, but that was in the past and her job was to make things better for the future. I liked her approach. She asked for advice and support. I did not promise anything, but I was feeling less angry.

The teacher proceeded to call every parent. When we arrived at the school on Monday night and met this warm, caring, and friendly teacher, we decided on the spot that we "loved" her and all would be well. And it was.

It seems like she acted totally on her own without the principal's suggestion or interference. She anticipated a problem and diffused the anger before the meeting. She asked for a little time to earn it with the kids, and she kept in touch with us.

That is what a great teacher does. They get on with the job.

Needless to say, Keith's future was not in any way impacted by this experience. He grew up, went to teachers college, and has become a brilliant special-education specialist. It fills me with great pride that, given my long history in education, my son chose this profession and has excelled at it.

How It All Began

I was a mediocre student in high school. My high school, Lawrence Park Collegiate, had a great track record of most students going on to university. If students were not doing well at Christmastime, it was often suggested they take Grade 13 over two years. My Botany and Zoology teacher, Douglas Penny, who also served as my Grade 13 advisor, suggested I switch to the two-year programme. He even indicated that, based on what I had done to date, I would probably not be successful at university.

I was devastated. I talked to my parents. We agreed that I should still pursue the one-year plan. My marks at the end of the second term were not much better. That year, to discourage students from writing the provincial standardized exams unless they were going to pass, a $5 fee was required for students to write the exam if they did not have a mark of 35 percent. Mr. Penny put my marks for both Botany and Zoology as under 35, even though my marks were in the low 40s. I thought that unfair and told my parents that I would show him. And I paid the $10 to write those final exams. Sad to say, I failed both subjects. In fact, I failed most subjects badly and did not pass Grade 13.

Discouraged, I was not certain as to next steps. I did apply to the Business School at Ryerson Institute of Technology (now Metropolitan Toronto University). In those days, we called it Rye High, as it was where you went if you could not get into university. Ryerson turned me down. I then heard that, because of the overwhelming number of students applying to Ryerson, for one year only, they would offer the first year of the Ryerson Business School at two Toronto high schools. Northern Secondary School was quite close, so I took off to meet with the principal, George Rawson. We had a pleasant conversation. Then he looked at me and said, "Gordon, your marks do not make you a good prospect. But I like your attitude. I will take a risk and admit you. Prove me right!" I loved him and I made the honour role.

It struck me then, and still does, that what a teacher says to you can affect your whole life.

Years later I had two degrees, was teaching graduate school at OISE, and had been recently elected as chair of the Toronto Board of Education. I was invited to speak on a panel at a major teachers' federation conference on the topic of community involvement in schools. Also speaking on the panel was none other than Douglas Penny, who by then was the assistant deputy minister of education. I had waited to meet up with him all these years! When we met prior to the panel starting, he looked at me and said, "Have we ever met?" *Have we ever met?* I thought he must be kidding! But no, he had absolutely no recollection of me.

But I sure remembered him! During my speech, I talked about the profound impact teachers can have on students. I told my story about my Grade 13 experience with Mr. Penny. I tried to keep it a bit light by saying that obviously back at Lawrence Park he did not think I would wind up where I was now. And, clearly, I did not think he would ever be an assistant deputy minister of education! After the panel, we went out and had a coffee and talked about this. Somehow, I had broken through, but for many others, a teacher's negative words could keep a young person down forever.

For me, the hero was George Rawson. When I was running the group home and George Rawson had retired as principal, I would have our kids meet with him before they started school. He made them feel better about themselves and about school too.

Elections — Stories from the Campaign Trail

I ran in six elections, won five, and lost one. And I have knocked on doors in many other campaigns, and still do. There is an excitement and energy in all campaigns, more so when you are winning! While policy is important, often what makes the difference is the personal connection to the voter.

Six Stories

Story 1: Big Yellow School Bus

One always remembers the first campaign...

My interest in education politics began during my School of Social Work placement at Niagara Public School during 1967 and 1968. My supervisor, Bob Chandler, thought it would be instructive to attend a Board of Education meeting. I was fascinated by it and started to follow the activities of the board in the press.

In early 1969, there was to be a meeting of the board, but there was no quorum. The diligent *Toronto Star* found out why ... seven school trustees were attending the Pacific Island Music Convention in Honolulu, Hawaii.

In those days, trustees did not need board approval to attend conferences.

Well, all hell broke loose. The *Toronto Star* immediately sent a reporter to Hawaii to interview the trustees and ask them why they were there. My local trustee, Alan Archer, was creative in answering that he "wanted to see how the ukulele could assist the inner-city reading programme"!

That was enough to motivate me to get involved! Also, after I started at Opportunity House, I realized that part of the problem might not be our kids, but the school system itself. I wish I could say many individuals and local parent-teacher associations approached me to run. Not so … I got up one morning and decided I was running. I was twenty-five.

I called my friend John Piper and off we went to get me elected. We wanted to champion several important inner-city issues but realized that the key for a newcomer was to get my name known. We brought together some old friends and raised a little money to produce a brochure but realized that we could not afford an office. John came up with the terrific idea of buying a used yellow school bus, putting my name on it, and driving through Ward 7 day and night. The bus cost $400, and our friend Al Sylvester kept fixing it. We got known very fast! The one problem was school kids who got on the bus and then did not want to get off to go to class.

June Callwood, the wonderful social activist, endorsed me. Judy Gardiner, a social work friend of mine, talked to her dad (George Gardiner, who founded the Gardiner Ceramic Museum). He called John Bassett at the *Toronto Telegram*, and the next thing I knew, I was endorsed by that paper. I had no idea things happened like that!

We were doing quite well when, suddenly, with just a few days left in the campaign, I was admitted to Wellesley Hospital with a painful kidney stone.

In those days, elections were held on a Monday in early December. John Piper had this idea that we should have a car parade through the ward on the Saturday morning before the election. He organized a bunch of cars and managed to get me out of the hospital for a couple of hours. I was to sit in this small, borrowed convertible and smile and wave to the people. The problem was that it was really cold and there were very few people out and about that early in the morning. John decided that what we should do was drive through the newly built high-rises in St. James Town. These buildings were being marketed in those days for "swinging singles." He said we would honk our horns, and people would come out on their balconies and wave. It did not quite work out that way.

Later that afternoon, my mom and her friends from the bridge club were working a phone bank to call people in St. James Town and remind them to vote on the Monday, and to mention that I had been through St. James Town earlier that morning. That approach changed very quickly when the first person said, "I will vote for anyone but that yahoo who came through with a group of people in cars honking their horns loudly!" The phone campaign ended very abruptly, and I went back to the hospital.

That Monday night, we celebrated victory, and Alan Archer finished way back. I received a call from Bob Strupat, a reporter with the *Toronto Star*, congratulating me. He asked what my first initiative would be. In my excitement, I said, "I am going to start a revolution!" There was a pause, and then Mr. Strupat said something like, "Mr. Cressy, I know this may be your first interview, and far be it for me, a reporter, to give you advice, but you may wish to rephrase your statement. Something more like 'I am going to improve the programme for inner-city kids' might work better. Not sure that you planning to start a revolution is the way to go."

Good advice that. And I will always be grateful to Bob Strupat.

Story 2: Losing

In the fall of 1976, I received a call from a person in Stuart Smith's office requesting twenty-minute meeting at his office. By that time I had been a school trustee and chair of the Toronto Board and was a pretty high-profile politician in Toronto. Stuart Smith was the leader of the Ontario Liberal Party. At that time, I was not a member of any party. I went to the meeting, and he asked me to run in the upcoming election for the Liberals in St. David riding.

Coincidentally, around the same time, I received a direct call from Stephen Lewis, the charismatic leader of the NDP. He asked me to meet with him for two hours at a place and time of my choosing. We talked at length, and I made the decision to run for the NDP in St. David, a riding that encompassed Rosedale in the north and Regent Park in the south.

Stephen Lewis and Gordon Cressy campaigning together.

It is a good lesson — who asks and how you ask can make all the difference.

Bill Davis, then Ontario premier, was leading a minority Progressive Conservative government. I was up against Margaret Scrivener, a cabinet minister. The Liberal candidate was Robert McClelland.

It was an exciting campaign; we had lots of volunteers and many people were crossing party lines to work for us. We had this neat sign that said, "We are working to elect Gordon Cressy." On some lawns, the "We" was crossed out and replaced by the word "I." Clearly, we caused some internal family tension!

Our strategy was to convince the south end of the riding (south of Bloor St.) that we were going to win. This turned out to be very effective, as we won that part of the riding by over 2,000 votes. Looking back, however, the mistake we made was to convince the north end that we might just win too, and people came out in droves to vote Conservative. In the end, the Liberal vote collapsed, and Robert McClelland received only 14 percent of the vote. Margaret Scrivener got 44 percent of the vote and I got 42 percent. We lost by 845 votes.

It was a very difficult loss. I didn't sleep much that night. The next morning, I woke early and went down to pick up the newspaper. There was a handwritten letter in the mailbox from Walter Gordon, a high-profile Liberal and the former federal minister of finance. He lived in the riding, and I had met him a couple of times but did not really know him. His note simply said that he had voted for me, and that defeat comes hard; but he knew I would rise again. It was a powerful message.

I learned a simple lesson. When you win, everyone wants to congratulate you and be your friend. When you lose, not so many people call. Walter Gordon taught me the importance of reaching out to people who have lost. Four years later, Ian Scott, the brilliant lawyer and Liberal candidate, ran against the same Margaret Scrivener and lost a close election. That night I dropped a handwritten note off at his house. He appreciated it a lot. He won the next election and became an outstanding attorney general.

Story 3: Sing-Alongs Do Work

In 1978, popular New Democrat John Gilbert, who had represented the federal Broadview riding since 1965, stepped down to become a judge. This meant a by-election was needed to fill the seat. At the time,

I was a member of Toronto City Council and was asked to chair the NDP nomination meeting.

There were four candidates. Kay McPherson, a highly regarded peace activist and former head of the National Action Committee on the Status of Women; John Harney, a university professor who had run in several NDP campaigns; Richard Johnston, a young activist who later became an MPP and president of Centennial College; and twenty-nine-year-old lawyer and former U of T student council member and activist Bob Rae. There was a large turnout out at the meeting and, much to many people's surprise, Bob Rae won on the first ballot.

Bob's sister Jennifer lived in the riding and was one terrific organizer. Her two daughters were friends with my two daughters, Jennifer and Jill. When the election came around, I told Bob that since I had represented a part of the riding for six years, I would be happy to help him out. The Conservative candidate was Tom Clifford, who had represented the riding as both school trustee and alderman for many years. He had run federally once before and finished a respectable second. The Liberal candidate was Philipp Varelis, who was not well known.

The NDP had held the riding for many years and had a strong ground game. Tom Clifford was well known and Bob Rae was not. Tom Clifford was a member of the Simpson Street United Church choir. He did well in the seniors' buildings and provided seniors with euchre scoresheets with his name printed on the back. I believe the Conservatives thought these seniors' buildings would lead them to victory. Bob was then, and is now, a serious musician. We thought it might be fun to try a sing-along in one those buildings.

The first sing-along was a great success, so we did more of them. Bob then brought his grandmother, Nell, along, and she sang Scottish songs with the residents. We then went from building to building, putting on sing-alongs featuring Bob Rae on the piano. People came in large numbers. Bob let them know who he was, but he did not need to talk policy. We all just sang and had a very good time.

On election night, October 16, 1978, Bob Rae beat Tom Clifford by just over 300 votes. It was that close. Bob went on to win twelve election campaigns after that, but none was as close as his first one.

Sing-alongs by their nature are upbeat and encourage people to participate. And in 1978, Bob Rae's sing-alongs may just have won him the by-election.

Story 4: Personal Warmth Carries the Day

In 1978, there was also a federal by-election in Rosedale riding, which went from Rosedale, north of Bloor, all the way south to the waterfront and included Regent Park.

David Crombie, the popular Toronto mayor, was running for the Conservatives; and John Evans, the highly regarded president of the University of Toronto, was running for the Liberals. The Liberals had held this riding for many years, with former cabinet minister Donald Macdonald having a towering presence. The NDP candidate, Ron Thompson, was a likeable person, but this election was to be fought out between Crombie and Evans. There was talk that, if John Evans won, he would be a natural successor to Pierre Trudeau. The media was all over this campaign, predicting a very close result.

On City Council, I represented the lower half of the riding and had a front-row seat to the campaign. There was an all-candidates meeting in Regent Park, and I arrived a little early to watch the crowd.

John Evans arrived a little early as well and walked over to an elderly lady he had met while canvassing. I stood close by, eavesdropping. He remembered meeting her and, more impressive, remembered that they had talked about the Christian Resource Centre and its services in Regent Park.

A couple of minutes before the meeting was to start, David Crombie bounded into the room and came over to say hi to me. He noticed this elderly lady and went to her first, called her by her first name, Mildred, and gave her a great big hug. As the meeting was about to begin, I went over to Mildred and asked who she was going to vote for. She smiled and told me, "David Crombie because he gave me a big hug." It was then that I knew that the campaign was over for John Evans. And it was. David Crombie won a decisive victory. Now eighty-seven years old and still bounding into rooms, David continues to give me and many others a big hug. I like it.

Story 5: Roti and the Trinidad Connection

In 1980, I was running a joint campaign for Toronto City Council with my friend David Reville. In those days, two aldermen were elected in each ward. In Ward 7, which included the high-rise St. James Town complex, we were going door to door. We would start at the top floor of these high-rises and work our way down to the bottom.

We were on the twentieth floor when I stopped to chat with a woman from Trinidad. Turns out we knew a couple of the same people from my time there. I could smell curry cooking in the kitchen and I told her that what I really missed was roti. She said she was making roti and asked if I would like one. I told her that would be FANTASTIC and that she had made my day. She wrapped it up nicely, gave it to me, and to top it off said, "I am going to vote for you." I put the roti in my pocket and continued canvassing. A few floors later, I met a man from Trinidad. We talked back and forth about how we missed the warm weather of Trinidad. He then said, "You know what I really miss?" I asked what, and he simply said, "Roti." I put my hand in my pocket, pulled out the roti, and said, "This is for you!" He was amazed. He said, "This is a miracle! I will vote for you! My friends will vote for you too!"

As we left the man's apartment, my friend David Reville turned and said, "This is too much! I cannot compete with this!" We were both elected but, as David predicted, I got more votes than he did.

Story 6: Calypso Connection

In 2018, my son Joe Cressy was running for Toronto City Council. My other son, Keith, and I were out knocking on doors for him. We met an older Black couple on their porch. We talked a bit back and forth, and I discovered they were from Grenada. I mentioned that I had lived in nearby Trinidad and Tobago for a few years. She told me her brother had gone to Trinidad as a young man and had done quite well as a calypso singer. I asked her his name. She said, "Oh, I don't think you would know him." I said, "Try me," and she said, "The Mighty Bomber." I was blown away as, outside of the Mighty Sparrow and Lord Kitchener, he was my favourite Calypsonian! So I responded, "The Mighty Bomber? Calypso King 1964, with the wonderful calypso song 'Joan and James'?" And then I proceeded to sing the first two verses of that stunningly great calypso. She began to cry. She said, "No white person in Canada knows that song! I will vote for your son. My husband and daughter will vote for him too!" Two days later I came and drove her and her husband to the advance poll to vote. She had told all her friends how I knew the song her brother had made famous in Trinidad. She told them to vote for my son too.

My son did win the election.

The Gay Bath House Raids, 1981

An Outsider Looks In

On the evening of February 5, 1981, at about 11:00 p.m., approximately 150 police officers swooped in and arrested close to 300 men as "found-ins" at four Toronto bath houses. They did huge damage, using crowbars and sledgehammers. The treatment of those individuals arrested was shockingly inappropriate.

The next day, 4,000 people demonstrated. There was a rumour, encouraged by the *Toronto Sun*, that the names of the people arrested would be made public. Ironically, to this day, it is alleged that two provincial cabinet ministers were arrested.

I had not been very active on gay issues, but every fibre of my being said this was wrong. Two of my fellow aldermen, Ron Kanter and Tom Clifford, and I went to visit the Richmond Street Health Emporium to see the damage for ourselves. We were greeted warmly by the owner, who toured us through the facilities and showed us the wanton destruction of walls, furniture, and windows. We were appalled.

A couple of days later, I hosted a press conference to raise our concerns about the raid. Others involved included longtime social activist June Callwood; the head of the Canadian Civil Liberties

Association, Alan Borovoy; and lawyer Morris Manning. By then, a chorus of voices was calling on the provincial government to call a formal enquiry into the Bath House Raids. On February 16, Reverend Brent Hawkes, the minister at Metropolitan Toronto Community Church, started a hunger strike, demanding a public inquiry.

The provincial government was having no part of this and said just that.

Earlier in this book, I mentioned that Kevin Ackroyd, the stepson of Jack Ackroyd, had lived in our group home. By this time, Jack was the chief of police in Toronto. I had come to know Jack and his family well and decided to call him directly for an off-the-record conversation. I got right to the point, asking him to tell me why these raids had taken place.

His answer: "Money laundering." I was stunned! I shot back with, "If it was money laundering, why did you go in at eleven p.m. rather than at nine in the morning and arrest just a few people?" His answer has stayed with me. He simply said, "Gordon, it was not my call."

The elusive question as to who made the call remains. Jack and I talked many times after that when we were both involved with the Toronto YMCA, but this call was never revisited.

For many years, the rumour was that Attorney General Roy McMurtry was involved in making the call that initiated those raids. I have known Roy well for over forty years and the idea of him making this call is just not consistent with the man I know and respect. He has said he was not involved. The puzzle of who made the call remains.

The protests continued to mount in a variety of settings, from the 519 Church Street Community Centre to formal presentations at the Police Services Board. More people outside the gay and lesbian community stepped forward, including writer Margaret Atwood; head of the Toronto Labour Council, Wally Majesky; Reverend Clifford Elliot of Bloor St. United Church; and twelve members of the Greater Toronto Rabbis.

It was clear then that this issue was not going away. On February 26, at City Council, two fellow aldermen, Pat Sheppard and David White, presented a detailed report entitled "Police Raids on Gay Steam Baths: On the Raids and Their Impact." They called for a public inquiry into the bath raids and added, "It would also be most appropriate and timely for the Inquiry to comment on relations between the Police and the gay community and recommend how these relations might be given to revising police policies to make an explicit statement regarding no discrimination based on sexual orientation as well as the establishment of an ongoing and permanent liaison between the Police and the Gay Community." City Council adopted their recommendations.

However, due to the continued lack of response by the provincial government, Brent was still on his hunger strike, and we were getting increasingly concerned about his health. We needed to find a resolution that would allow him to end his strike. Quiet conversations were held with Dr. Daniel Hill, the well-respected founding head of the Ontario Human Rights Commission and the mayor's advisor on community and race relations, to ask him to conduct a study. On March 12, City Council passed a resolution to proceed with this study and to ask Dr. Hill to do it.

This was not the provincial inquiry that had been advocated, but it was enough to end Brent's strike. Dr. Hill, however, declined, saying that he had too many other commitments to give this pressing study the time and urgency it deserved. He approached lawyer Arnold Bruner to do the study.

Arnold went diligently to work and built a degree of trust with both the police and the gay community. His seminal report, entitled "Out of the Closet, a Study of Relations between the Homosexual Community and the Police," came out on September 24, 1981. Today, as 2SLGBTQI+ rights have correctly emerged across Canada, this report looks somewhat antiquated. But at the time, it was a major stepping stone to getting us where we are today.

United Way Stories

Getting There

I was in my second term as the senior alderman for Ward 7. I had been elected to the City Executive Committee and was viewed by some as a bit of a rising star. In the fall of 1981, we had formed a small committee to explore the possibility of me running for mayor in the election scheduled for the fall of 1982. Art Eggleton had defeated John Sewell in the 1980 election, but he had yet to emerge as a strong mayor.

I must admit that I did not want the job badly. Seems to me, you must feel these things deep in your belly. One afternoon, Don Richmond, the commissioner of Social Services, told me he had received a call about the ongoing search for a new president of the United Way of Greater Toronto. He said they were having difficulty finding the right person, and he might apply. In those days, the United Way was viewed as a bit of a sleepy organization.

A light went on immediately, and I thought, *That job is for me!* Politics is essentially adversarial, and I realized that I was much more interested in connecting people to get things done.

I went home that evening and wrote out my resume by hand. The next morning, I took it down to Al Beech, the head of the consulting firm doing the search. We met briefly and I told him, "I am your guy! I have been preparing for this job all my life."

He took me seriously, and many interviews later, I was hired. I discovered later that the United Way's search committee wrestled at length with my appointment, mainly due to concerns about hiring a member of the NDP. Finally, Allan Slaight, who became a dear friend and mentor, cast the deciding vote saying, "Cressy, high risk, high potential — I go with potential!"

And that was that. I was hired to be a change agent, lift the profile of the United Way, raise more dollars, and not ruffle too many feathers along the way. I had a lot to learn.

A few years back, well-known Toronto magician David Ben, also a friend of Allan's, wrote a book about Allan with the neat title *Slaight: Off Hand*. David referred to Allan's involvement with the United Way and mentioned that phrase, "high risk, high potential." On one of my visits to Allan, I asked how he thought I had done, some thirty-five years later. He looked at me with a mischievous smile and said, "Cressy, the jury is still out!"

Announcing My Appointment

There was a large press conference to announce my appointment.

Family, friends, politicians, and United Way senior officials were all there.

It went well. I said the right things. I thanked people for coming and said I was ready to embrace and grow the United Way.

The next morning a headline in the *Toronto Star* screamed out, **"Head of United Way to Receive $80,000."** I was devasted and immediately sought a correction, for it was not $80,000 but $75,000!

It did not matter. The point was made. The fact that whoever got the job was going to be paid that amount was irrelevant. The salary was perceived as outlandishly high in the social services field. People wrote letters to the editor saying they would not give to the United Way again.

The United Way was a big job and should be paid accordingly.

But that did not help. For the next couple of months press articles would lead with "$75,000-a-year head of the United Way, Gordon Cressy, says..."

It really got to me as I had not taken the job based on salary.

Sleepless, I woke Joanne up in the middle of the night and said that I was going to recommend that the board reduce my salary to $50,000. She made it clear to me that this was a mistake! Joanne knows how to do that.

Undaunted, I went and told the senior United Way staff that I was thinking of doing this. They too made it very clear to me not to go down this road.

We decided our task was to earn the trust of the people and raise significantly more dollars. Over the next few years, we succeeded and the story faded away, but not completely.

A store owner in my old political ward put up a huge sign criticizing me and suggesting people not give to the United Way. A couple of times I asked him to take it down but to no avail.

A year later, we were in a van with new United Way board members touring United Way agencies. We passed by the sign, and everyone was upset, particularly me. Peter Bronfman asked why the store owner did not take down the sign and I told him because it was his building and he just would not do it.

Then Peter said something that has stayed with me all these years. "Buy the building." That is one of the things about the rich. They often think differently than the rest of us. Two years later, the owner finally took the sign down and put up a new sign attacking someone else.

Do Not Let Your Uniform Block Your Message

Before my official start at the United Way, the board chair, David Lewis, who was CEO of Continental Bank, took me out to dinner on a cold winter evening. We went to Winston's, then a very high-end restaurant in downtown Toronto. I was not sure why we were there. We had a pleasant dinner; it turned out that he knew my father from earlier banking days.

As we started dessert, he looked at me and said he wanted to talk to me about my parka. I was a bit taken aback. Like, what about my parka? I knew it was old and more than a little worse for wear. He said, "Gordon, I don't think you could get a job as a parking-lot attendant with that parka." He then asked me if I owned a suit. I admitted that I did not have one.

The purpose of the dinner became clear. He said everyone quite liked my brown corduroy jacket, that it might work well in a union hall or academic setting, but we were going to be meeting with the top CEOs in Canada, and a suit was in order. His exact words were, "I don't want your uniform to block your message."

Off I went to Harry Rosen's. Harry even measured me himself, and I bought a suit and a blue blazer. Harry called it the workhorse of the wardrobe.

David Lewis's advice has followed me my whole career, and I understood the need to dress for the arena I was in.

Changing the Board — Diversity Matters

Back in 1982, there was not much talk about diversity. But it was clear to me that we needed to change the face of the United Way, and quickly. The board was virtually all white and did not reflect the changing Toronto population. Toronto was rapidly becoming a multiracial city, but the board of the United Way was not.

The executive committee also functioned as the nominating committee. One morning I was amazed that the whole committee arrived for the meeting at the same time. I asked how that had happened. The answer was simple ... everyone lived on or around Inglewood Drive in north Rosedale! They were all good people, but the composition of the board needed to change.

When I raised the question of bringing people from different backgrounds to the table they said that was my job. So off I went to see my friend Dr. Joseph Wong.

I had come to know Joseph a bit through his work with the Vietnamese boat people in the late 1970s. More important, I had watched his considerable organizing skills after CTV's *W5* released an episode called "Campus Giveaway" with the stunningly inappropriate subtitle, "Why the Chinese Are Taking Our Places at the University." The show was clearly racist. Over nine months, Joseph worked with both the Chinese and the broader community to get CTV to reverse its position. Finally, at a banquet attended by 1,500 people, CTV apologized for its portrayal of Chinese Canadians and followed up with a special about the enormous Chinese contribution to Canadian society, including building the railway across Canada. I clearly remember Joseph thanking those who were there at the beginning, nine months earlier, as well as those who had just joined last week. Joseph said everyone was welcome.

I wanted Joseph to join the United Way Board, and I thought I made a compelling ask. Joseph simply said that the United Way did not serve the Chinese community. He said that if we were truly interested, that he would organize a meeting in the Chinese community, that the discussion would be in Cantonese, that he would provide a translator, and that the chair of the board of the United Way should attend. This way we would learn how to serve the Chinese community. I went back to the board with this proposal. I remember one of our members saying, "You mean we have to go out to bring people in?" Yes indeed. That is what community organizing is all about.

The meeting was held, and Joseph Wong joined the board. Others did too — people like Al Hamilton from *Contrast Newspaper*, which serves the Black community; and Kappu Desai, a South Asian community leader. Al Hamilton commented, "We are at the table now, but not the head table yet." More on the transformation of the United Way later...

Joseph Wong filled many roles on the United Way Board and eventually became the chair. A couple years later, Joseph began his quest to create a culturally appropriate nursing home for Chinese seniors. There are now four such homes in the Greater Toronto Area, and the Yee Hong Centres for Geriatric Care are now the world-recognized gold standard for seniors' care. But at the beginning, it was just Joseph and a few of his friends. He came to me and suggested that I come on the board. I asked why would he want me to join the board of a Chinese nursing home? He answered, "We need a white person!" I went on the board.

Chairing the Campaign

The key to any successful fundraising campaign is strong volunteer leadership. The phrase that you need a "champion" to lead is absolutely true. Quite frankly, the United Way was in the doldrums. No new agencies had been admitted in several years. We were starting our annual campaign shortly, and had been unable to attract a senior business leader to chair it. Janet MacInnis, a longtime and dedicated board member, stepped in and agreed to chair the campaign.

The next year, I got out early to recruit a campaign chair. I must have had about five rejections. I went to see John Black Aird, who was the lieutenant governor of Ontario and the honorary chair of the United Way. He was a friend of my parents and, when I was hired, he had called me and offered to help. If anyone ever says that to you, mark it down and follow up.

So off I went to see John Aird. I told him about my difficulty in recruiting a campaign chair. He politely asked what the responses had been to my request. I told him they had all been the same. They liked the United Way and wanted to help, but they were too busy, and they would be pleased to provide their retiring vice president of some department to lead the campaign. John looked at me and said, "Gordon, you are a nice young fellow, but to be frank, you have no clout. Here is how we are going to do it. I will come, two important customers of the person you want to recruit will come, you can come too, and the person will say yes."

We decided to recruit David McCamus, the new president of Xerox. It turned out that he had volunteered at the Elliott Donnelley Youth Center in Chicago when he worked there with Xerox. A remarkable coincidence! We trooped into his office: John Aird, two Xerox customers, and me. I clearly remember David getting up from his desk, putting his hands in the air, and saying, "I don't know why you are here but the answer is yes!"

David was a sensational chair. We raised more money than ever before and started funding new agencies for the first time in years, including a number from diverse communities. And we set a standard for campaign chairs that has continued to this day.

The United Way and Conrad Black

In the summer of 1982, just after I started at the United Way, Doug Bassett, then head of CTV, agreed to do a television special on the United Way free of charge. We were all excited, as this would help in the rebuilding of the United Way. During the special, Conrad Black was interviewed. He mentioned that, many years earlier, his father had played a role in setting up the United Way (then called the Community Chest). He indicated that he was a strong supporter of the United Way. I was intrigued by this and asked our data people about the size of Conrad Black's donation. Imagine my surprise to discover that he had given only $100!

I called Conrad Black and asked to meet with him. He was gracious when I arrived at his office and told his secretary he did not want to be interrupted. I was impressed.

I asked him directly about the size of his donation. He said he was home one evening when a canvasser for the United way knocked on his door. He asked her what was the largest donation she had received that evening, and she said $50. Conrad said he would double it. She was pleased and went on to the next door.

At that moment, we decided to end the door-to-door canvass and focus on the workplace as our major source of funds!

As we discussed the United Way, Conrad had an idea of how he could be helpful — in addition to increasing the size of his donation. He told me he was very close to Cardinal Emmett Carter and he served on the board of Share Life, the fundraising arm of Catholic Charities. Catholic Charities had been part of the United Way for many years, but established Share Life in reaction to the United Way's decision to admit Planned Parenthood as a member agency. Planned Parenthood's position on abortion was unacceptable to the Catholic Church.

Conrad suggested that there might be a way to merge Share Life back into the United Way, and that this would be good for the community. Conrad mentioned that the highly regarded Cardinal Joseph Bernardin from Chicago was still a strong United Way supporter, even though the United Way had admitted Planned Parenthood as a member agency.

Off I went to Chicago (my old stomping ground) to meet with Cardinal Bernardin. He was welcoming and charming. He had a simple solution to the problem of Catholic Charities' difficulty with Planned Parenthood doing abortion referrals. He said that the United Way in Chicago had set a new policy that not one cent from any Catholic donor would ever go to Planned Parenthood. I inquired how the United Way could implement such a policy. He smiled kindly and said he had no idea and had no desire to find out. The meeting ended and I returned to Toronto all the wiser.

Conrad Black then set up a meeting at Cardinal Carter's home in Rosedale with me; Paul Godfrey, who was chair of Metropolitan Toronto Council; and himself. I arrived first and had an enjoyable chat with Cardinal Carter, mentioning that my wife had had a wonderful experience as a boarder at the Sacred Heart Convent School in Montreal. Paul Godfrey arrived shortly thereafter, and we waited and waited for Conrad Black. Finally, an hour later, there was a knock on the door. Conrad apologized for being late, saying that he had to drop his wife off at the hospital. Cardinal Carter looked hard at Conrad and said, "The pope never kept me waiting for a meeting." Conrad responded, "Well, the pope does not have a wife!" Point made!

We then went on to the purpose of the meeting. I reported on my discussion with Cardinal Bernardin, and that it seemed to be working. Cardinal Carter listened intently and said he would think about it and get back to us. He then added that, if Catholic Charities came back in, they would want to negotiate a higher percentage of the funds than when they left. Hmm. I wondered to myself if this was the real motive for perhaps reuniting the agencies!

A few weeks later, Cardinal Carter came back and said that the priests did not want to pursue a merger, and the discussion ended. Conrad was more than upset and made the point to me that, if Cardinal Carter had wanted this to happen, it would have happened. Conrad resigned from the board of Share Life. Today, some forty-five years later, both organizations still exist. The United Way has grown by about eight times and Share Life by about three times.

The United Way, Sounds United, and Allan Slaight

In 1986, we recruited Allan Slaight, CEO of Standard Broadcasting, to chair the campaign. Allan was an entrepreneur, philanthropist, broadcaster, promotor, and lover of magic. He was also very funny. He wanted to make the United Way fun and exciting. He and his son Gary enlisted their friends in the media and the entertainment world.

They came up with the idea of Sounds United, an evening when the entertainment and media industry would come together, dress up, and lip synch well-known songs. The media loved it, as they were recognizing their own. We raised significant money and lifted the profile of the United Way at the same time.

We were also looking for a way to re-engage young people. Allan and Gary suggested we have a mainstream rock band preform at Maple

Leaf Gardens. He suggested Rush, who were still in their early days. They had already sold out Maple Leaf Gardens for two nights and, with their manager Ray Daniels, agreed to do a third show for us. Next, we went off to see Harold Ballard at the Gardens. Despite his reputation as a curmudgeon, he was quite generous. He agreed to give us the Gardens for free on two conditions — one, that others involved with the concert would donate their time and/or money; and two, that we not say anything nice about him in public! We readily agreed.

John Piper was our director of communications, community relations, and special events. He and Allan Slaight hit it off immediately. John headed off to meet with the International Alliance of Theatrical Stage Employees. They agreed on the spot to a cheque swap, whereby they would be paid the night of the event and immediately sign over the cheque as a donation to the United Way. Michael Cohl, head of Ticketmaster, agreed to waive their fees; the Police and Fire Service agreed to waive their fees, and we were on.

Rush was FANTASTIC and, just as important, in the middle of the concert they stopped and talked to the kids about the importance of the campaign and how they should support the United Way in their schools. And they did.

Allan's 1986 campaign was a resounding success. Even to this day, that campaign had the largest year-over-year percentage increase.

Allan Slaight and Gordon Cressy.

Cutting Expenses

When I was hired, a reservation expressed to me by the hiring committee was that I had limited experience in managing budgets, and that I needed to show that I could control expenses.

I had two early experiences — one worked, the other not so much.

The first was our advertising budget. It turned out that we were paying a lot of money for print media, TV commercials, and radio advertisements. More than that, we were paying for actors and actresses. Allan Slaight would have none of it. He said, "Use real people. They will tell their own story, and it would be more powerful." He also thought it would be stupid — that is the word he used — to go back to Doug Bassett of CTV and say thanks for the free television, but this year we are going to cut the amount of advertising we purchase at your station.

Better to bring all the media together in one room and say to them, "This is your United Way, and you have a responsibility to promote it." We cut out the advertising budget entirely and got more support from the media than ever before.

A few years later, one of our board members suggested we go to the banks, who had already done their advertising "buys," and suggest they give us some of their spots. They agreed, but they wanted no recognition for this as they did not want to do it for any other charity.

My second foray into cost control did not go so well. I found we could get a different telephone provider than Bell at a cheaper cost. I did the numbers and it was clear that over a five-year period we could save significant dollars. I was quite proud of myself as I prepared the proposal for our executive committee.

The day before the meeting, I received a call from Joe Cruden, a senior executive at Bell, whom I had known from political circles. He had caught wind of the proposed change in telephone providers.

He wanted to assure me that this would not alter Bell's corporate gift to the United Way. He added that the employees of Bell (one of the largest donor groups to the United Way) would be mighty disappointed to learn of the United Way changing its telephone provider, and he suspected that many Bell employees might no longer donate to the United Way.

At the executive meeting the next day, it was clear to me that a number of our members had received calls from Bell. It was suggested to me that I might like to withdraw this proposal. I did. Bell continues to this day to be a major supporter of the United Way. The other telephone provider went out of business a couple of years after our decision.

Raising the Big Dollars

The United Way was always a populist organization. We prided ourselves on receiving thousands upon thousands of small gifts and had never developed a campaign for larger gifts.

During my first few months on the job, I continued to serve on City Council, as I did not want to force a by-election, and I donated my city salary to the United Way. It turned out that this made me the largest individual donor to the United Way — at $12,000! That seemed weird to me.

I went off to meet with Steve Ain, the remarkably successful head of the United Jewish Appeal (UJA). He was shocked to hear this. He told me there were many significantly large donors to the United Jewish Appeal, and asked if I knew Phil Granovsky, the head of Atlantic Packaging. I told him that Phil had been on the committee that hired me at the United Way. He indicated that Phil made a very large annual gift to the UJA and suggested that I meet with him. It turns out that Phil was giving $1 million annually to the UJA and was part of a select group across North America that gave that amount each year.

I went to our trusty United Way records and discovered that Phil had given $2,500 the previous year. Armed with that information, off I went to meet with Phil Granovsky. We had a candid conversation about his gift. Then Phil turned to me and said, "Gordon, I am a wealthy man, but not as wealthy as the Bassetts, the Blacks, or the Eatons, and I can assure you they are not giving to the United Jewish

Appeal. When they are giving you $50,000 annually you come back and see me, and I will give you $50,000." Welcome advice that.

I went back. We brought some leaders together and moved our $1,000 "Leaders of the Way" campaign upward. After I left, Anne Golden, who took over and had a fabulous twelve-year run as president of the United Way, took leadership giving to a whole new level. She received the first $1 million gift from none other than Allan Slaight. That annual tradition of $1 million donors continues to this day.

Outreach

As we moved forward in expanding the United Way in the 1980s, it became clear that changing the face of the board, while a good beginning, was not enough.

So John Piper helped organize three strong advisory groups for the United Way, representing the South Asian community, the Chinese community, and the Black community. These groups were not about image and window dressing, but about making real change, including bringing in new member agencies from these and other communities. These groups felt that over the long term they would integrate into the United Way family, but in the short term there was work to be done. The groups decided to create events that would build pride in their communities and raise money for the United Way. Some of these individuals began serving on United Way committees, like allocations and finance.

The Chinese community, under the leadership of Joseph Wong, started the United Way Walkathon to launch our annual campaign. This launch event grew each year and involved member agencies as well as business and labour organizations. In addition to the walkathon, which involved all United Way member agencies and supporters, the Chinese advisory group wanted to do something distinctive in their community. They recruited Liu Dehai, one of the world's great classical pipa players, to perform at a benefit concert for the United Way. The pipa is a four-stringed Chinese instrument, often referred to as a lute. The music is hauntingly beautiful, and the concert was a great success. Money was raised, and more people came to know about the United Way.

Joseph Wong, me, and my son Joseph.

Emboldened by this success, the South Asian community embarked on a great adventure. They told us they wanted to bring Lata Mangeshkar to perform at Maple Leaf Gardens. I said I have never heard of her. Shows what I knew! Lata Mangeshkar had performed sold-out concerts all over the world, including twice at Maple Leaf Gardens. Yet the mainstream media in Toronto had never covered her performances.

Initial contacts were made with Lata Mangeshkar, and she indicated a willingness to do a benefit concert. John Piper went to India to confirm the details. In the end, Air India flew over a group of performers free of charge, led by Lata, her sister Usha, and the quite funny comedian and playback singer Kishore Kumar. The Royal York Hotel put the group up for free, and Harold Ballard once again gave us the Maple Leaf Gardens free of charge.

On Sunday, June 9, a beautiful evening, Lata and her group performed a sold-out concert at Maple Leaf Gardens. The audience was made up of a wide variety of people; the large majority were originally from India, Pakistan, Sri Lanka, Tanzania, Uganda, Kenya, Trinidad, and Guyana.

It was a magical evening. At the end of the show Lata played tribute to Anne Murray, singing Anne's famous song "You Needed Me." Again, money was raised, people were happy, and the United Way made new friends.

I was in a taxi the next day, heading to the airport. My South Asian taxi driver turned to me and asked, "Do you know who sang for the United Way last night?" (He had no idea who I was.) He didn't wait for me to answer. He had this beaming smile and said, "Lata Mangeshkar, and we are so proud." The headline on the front page of the *Toronto Star* said it best: "Lata Sings for Our United Way."

A few years later, someone had the idea that the United Way should host a fundraiser called the West Indies vs. the Rest of the World in Cricket. A feasibility study cast doubts about whether it would work. I mean cricket in Toronto … really? We went ahead anyway. Forty thousand people showed up, and over $500,000 was raised for the United Way. Once again, reaching out worked.

Bishop Desmond Tutu and Harry Belafonte Come to Toronto

The United Way's Black Development Committee, chaired by the remarkable Lloyd McKell from the Toronto Board of Education, was looking to host a signature event.

I had become aware that, in some cities in the United States, members of the Black community were becoming disenchanted with the United Way. There were moves to promote workplace giving to raise money for the Black United Fund. I did not want us going down that path.

The committee members, many of whom were seasoned activists, seized upon the idea of bringing Bishop Desmond Tutu to Toronto to talk about the struggle to end apartheid in South Africa. I remember going down to meet with Bishop Tutu in Boston. I first visited my daughter, Jennifer, in Connecticut, and we drove together to Boston to visit Bishop Tutu, a meaningful moment for both of us. Tutu greeted us warmly and said, "You have come all the way from Toronto to meet me," and then he gave me a hug. When I told him about the idea he simply said, "I will be there."

The Black Development Committee's plan was to host an "Arts Against Apartheid Festival," supported by the United Way. At this time, Nelson Mandela was still in jail, apartheid in South Africa was still government policy, and Black South Africans were still suffering under government-sponsored oppression.

When the festival idea first became public, it was met with both excitement and apprehension. The excitement came from community members. The concern was expressed foremost by a columnist with the *Toronto Sun* who questioned why the United Way would have anything to do with Archbishop Tutu, describing him as a troublemaker and maybe even a communist. Some corporate leaders wondered aloud why we would have an outsider come to Toronto, though they did not raise that concern about Lata Mangeshkar. She was, after all, just a singer.

Opposition was growing, and it looked like I might be in trouble with the United Way Board. A fundamental lesson I have learned is that, if you lose the confidence of your board, you are finished. Yet to me, this initiative was fundamentally important.

Enter Lieutenant Governor John Aird. He, you will remember, helped me in our recruitment of David McCamus, and we had become friends. He called my wife and said, "I see that your husband is in a bit of trouble here." But he quickly added that he believed I was doing the right thing. As the honorary chair of the United Way, he was eligible to attend meetings of the board and executive committee. He had never come to any of these meetings, usually just showing up at our annual meeting. He said he would show up at the next few board meetings and sit beside me and, in effect, hold my hand. He did just that. He did not speak, but people knew why he was there.

John suggested that we find some allies in the corporate world, so I went off to see David McCamus. I knew, based on his push for outreach and his volunteer work with the Elliott Donnelley Youth Center in Chicago, that he would support this idea. But I also knew that it would be a risk for him to do this publicly. He called the next day to say that his head of public affairs, Peter Brophy, had suggested that he duck the issue. David said sometimes you must take a stand. And he did. Years later, when Nelson Mandela died, David called and said we were on the right side of history, and he was proud of being involved in the Toronto Arts Against Apartheid Festival, supported by the United Way.

John Piper rented an old van and we picked up David McCamus at his office, popular singer Salome Bey on a street corner, and other members of the Black Development Committee and headed down the QEW to Hamilton. Harry Belafonte was performing in Hamilton that evening, and we went to ask him to participate in the event. He agreed and said that he would perform twice for free at Massey Hall.

Meanwhile John Aird went to Premier David Peterson to inquire about the possibility of Archbishop Tutu addressing the provincial legislature. Peterson agreed, and Desmond Tutu did the address. He was given a standing ovation.

As the event grew, more people wanted to participate. The Arts Against Apartheid Festival went on from May 25 to June 1, 1986. It included a theatre show, literary readings, film and dance presentations, craft exhibits, a gala dinner attended by many dignitaries, and a two-evening concert at Massey Hall with many performers donating their time.

By the time the event was happening, even the *Toronto Sun* had come onside and celebrated this massive partnership. Business, labour, community leaders, faith communities, and politicians of all political stripes came to the gala. The head of the United Way of America, Bill Aramony, flew up for the event. The gala on Friday, May 30, was extraordinary. Bishop Tutu fired up the crowd with a stirring speech condemning apartheid. It was an important and powerful week for us all.

But despite all the goodwill, it was not all smooth sailing.

The performances by Harry Belafonte on the Saturday and Sunday were to be the icing on the cake. Harry was my idol. He sang Trinidad calypso songs with verve and gusto. His song "Don't Stop the Carnival," about Carnival in Trinidad, remains one of my all-time favourites.

During his first concert, he took us on a welcome trip down memory lane with favourites like "Island in the Sun," "Jamaica Farewell," "Banana Boat," and "Come Back Liza," and he even sang Leonard Cohen's famous "Suzanne." In the middle of the concert, as the honorary chair of the Toronto Arts Against Apartheid Festival, he spoke to everyone about the importance of the event in the struggle against apartheid. He congratulated the United Way for supporting this event, despite some opposing the United Way's involvement.

Then he departed from his prepared script and noted that some corporations in Toronto had not supported the event. He incorrectly stated that one of those companies was Eaton's. Then he said, "So don't shop at Eaton's!" I was thrown for a loop. After all, Harry was leaving town after the concert, and we at the United Way wanted and needed Eaton's support. As if that was not enough, for the rest of the concert Harry managed to find ways to knock Eaton's. During the song "Matilda," he had different parts of the audience sing different verses with him. In one of the verses, he asked women over forty to join him. At first no one joined in. Then he said, "Come on, women over forty — I am over forty! And you can use Oil of Olay ... but do not buy it at Eaton's!" The audience by and large ate it up. But I was more than a little upset that my hero had let me down.

I did not sleep much that night, worried that our relationship with Eaton's was hurt. It was a story in the press. The next morning, I called Harry and went to his hotel to explain that several companies had been initially skeptical of the United Way's involvement but had come onside and had supported us. He promised to make it right that night, so I invited Courtney Pratt, our remarkable board chair, and others to attend. Well, that night Harry not only told people not to shop at Eaton's but went on to suggest that people not shop or do banking at several more companies!

Harry left to much applause. On reflection, I think Harry's reference to shopping at Eaton's was part of his show routine … with him picking a local retailer in all his concerts. To Eaton's credit, the company remained a strong supporter of the United Way. Fifteen years later, John Craig Eaton was the chancellor of Ryerson University when Nelson Mandela and his wife, Graça Machel, received their honorary degrees. While I will always admire Harry Belafonte's music and his extraordinary commitment to social justice and human rights, on those two evenings, he played loose with the facts.

Although people like David McCamus and John Aird stand out, the real heroes of the event were Lloyd McKell and the Black Development Committee, who tenaciously dreamed up, pursued, and saw this festival through from start to finish.

Four short years later Nelson Mandela was released from prison.

LOCAL NEWS / FEBRUARY 10, 1988 share 3

COMMUNITY APPRECIATION: Representatives from Metro Toronto's Black and West Indian community gathered at the University of Toronto's Simcoe Hall, to pay tribute to Gordon Cressy (centre) past president of the United Way of Greater Toronto. Presenting Cressy with a plaque was Carmen Jens of the Jamaican Canadian Association. Photo by David Maylor

Did the Outreach Really Work?

It was a good beginning. New agencies were admitted, like the Riverdale Immigrant Women's Centre, Tropicana Community Services, and Chinese Interpreter Services. The board and all United Way committees began to better reflect the community. When I was leaving the United Way, the Black community presented me and the United Way with a plaque listing the new agencies we had admitted.

This is hard but important work, and much remains to be done. The United Way of today is continuing to meet this challenge head-on.

From Staff to Volunteer

1. The YMCA

As mentioned earlier, my first real job was working with CUSO to build the YMCA in Trinidad. When I returned to Canada, I got involved with both organizations as a volunteer. The YMCA was moving to involve more young people on its board, and I was appointed to the National YMCA Board in 1970. And in early 1973, I was named chair of the board of the National Council of YMCAs. How did this happen? I was a twenty-nine-year-old social worker! But I soon got the hang of chairing meetings and committees.

The World Alliance of YMCAs meets every four years. At its 1969 meeting, the alliance decided to have its 1973 meeting in Africa for the first time. They chose Uganda, as it seemed to be a stable developing country; however, in 1972, newly installed President Idi Amin expelled many South Asians. Nevertheless, we were encouraged by the leaders of other African countries, except for Julius Nyerere of Tanzania, to still go to Uganda. So our 15-person delegation from Canada travelled to Uganda by way of Egypt, Ethiopia, and Kenya.

We stayed in a big hotel in Kampala. We were more than a little surprised when Idi Amin showed up with his security guards in tow and joined us in the pool. He was very jovial and friendly.

For the first few days, we went to meetings with other delegates from around the world. I made a few new friends. I was particularly taken with Lij Endelkachew Makonnen, vice president of the International YMCA and the soon-to-be prime minister of Ethiopia. Turns out we had a mutual friend from my college days at George Williams College, Desta Girma. Desta had returned to Ethiopia after graduation and worked for the Ethiopian YMCA in Addis Ababa. Lij was aware trouble was brewing in his home country, but during his time at the conference, he was a master diplomat. We promised we would keep in touch after the conference ended.

We developed a new set of principles for the YMCA, which we called the Kampala Principles. Then we were invited to a luncheon banquet at the president's lodge. There was to be food and entertainment, and we all looked forward to going.

When we arrived, there were rows and rows of chairs, though the front row had only five chairs, and clearly one was for the president. I thought, *This is my time.* So I plonked myself down next to Idi Amin, and we spent the next three hours talking together and watching the entertainment. He argued that he did not dislike the South Asian community but thought it important for Africans to control their own affairs. He was encouraging people to go back to the land and farm rather than migrating into the cities where there was no work. These were his early days.

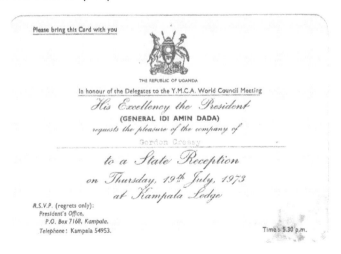

Idi Amin and me (with long hair and a moustache), July 1973.

Upon my return, my next-door neighbour Mike McIvor, a CityTV news reporter, thought people would want to hear about my time with Idi Amin. I went down to the studio and basically said nice things about Idi Amin. Big mistake — as shortly thereafter, he became a brutal dictator. My picture with him quickly went from the living room to the basement. And somewhere in the CityTV vault, there is a tape that shows me in a very negative light!

In the meantime, my friend Lij Endelkachew Makonnen became the prime minister of Ethiopia. People were revolting against the government, and in the spring of 1974, he was placed under house arrest. We in the Y were concerned for his safety, and I thought that the YMCAs across the world should rise up and secure his release. The U.S. argued for quiet diplomacy. Its voice carried the day. In November, Lij Endelkachew Makonnen and several government officials were executed.

A decade ago, I was working at Canadian Tire (more about this later). Canadian Tire had a special sale evening and asked most of us at head office to assist in local stores. I was sent to a store in Scarborough. Near the end of the evening, I was chatting with a young man who told me that he was born in Ethiopia. I told him the only person I knew from Ethiopia was Lij Endelkachew Makonnen. He looked stunned. Then, with tears in his eyes, he told me that Lij Endelkachew Makonnen was his father. We both cried and hugged. It was a riveting moment.

2. CUSO

In 1983, I was elected to chair the board of CUSO, which, in 1981, had changed its name from Canadian University Service Overseas. The reason for the name change was that the skill sets needed for placement overseas no longer applied just to university students. The average age of the volunteers was now over thirty.

This was an exciting time for CUSO. We expanded the board to include international members, the staff unionized, and rather than just sending Canadian volunteers overseas, we started to hire local people in their home countries.

We also started to fundraise, since the government was cutting back on its support for our programmes. This inevitably resulted in big debates about which companies we would and would not take money from. I knew we had a problem when twelve people signed up for the committee looking at companies that we did not want to accept money from, and only three signed up for the fundraising committee! We were pleased to learn that the Toronto Dominion Bank was the first major bank to divest its holdings of companies doing business in South Africa. We even said nice things about TD in public. Dick Thompson, the CEO, thanked us but suggested that our praise be somewhat quiet as many of the bank's customers did not agree with the bank's position!

Ronnie Thwaites, then a TV host and more recently the minister of education in Jamaica, was a new international board member. He was informed that there had been a raid by the police on the CUSO office in Kingston, Jamaica. He suggested I come down and help sort things out. It turns out that under Prime Minister Manley, CUSO in Jamaica had developed some close working relationships with Cuba. The new government under Prime Minister Edward Seaga did not take kindly to this. I travelled to Jamaica, and after a series of meetings, we managed to smooth things out.

While in Jamaica, we learned that one of our CUSO volunteers had been asked to leave the island of Dominica. A CUSO volunteer being kicked out of a country was unheard of, and Ronnie and I resolved to get to the bottom of it. We called the Canadian High Commission and asked them to get in touch with Eugenia Charles, the prime minister of Dominica. They were unsuccessful. Sometimes I've learned, just do it yourself. So I got on the phone and asked the long-distance operator to put me through to the prime minister of Dominica. Imagine my surprise when, a minute later, a voice comes on the line saying, "Eugenia Charles speaking."

I outlined the problem. She suggested we come to Dominica and meet with her. Ronnie and I flew to Barbados and then took the short LIAT flight to Dominica. We went straight from the airport to meet with Prime Minister Charles. We were ushered in immediately, served tea, and began our conversation. Prime Minister Charles, who had been educated at the University of Toronto, did not beat around the bush.

She told us that CUSO volunteers had been providing great service to the people of Dominica since the 1960s, and she was aware of CUSO's new initiative to hire local Dominicans where possible. She acknowledged that in principle this was a very good idea — but, in practice, not so much. Her powerful point was that, in a small island nation, it is almost impossible to be politically neutral. What that meant for Dominica was, of the eleven people working for CUSO, nine supported the opposition and only two supported the government.

She went on to say that her government had requested that CUSO send a Canadian nurse to work at the local hospital. She said that she had naively assumed that CUSO would send a blond-haired white nurse. But CUSO had sent down a Jamaican-Canadian Rastafarian nurse! To top it off, she supported the opposition! At that point, the prime minister said she had had enough and sent this young woman back to Canada!

Ronnie and I headed back to our homes. As we chatted, we realized that what happens on the ground is the real test of the success of the programme. As an aside, at the Barbados airport, I showed them my return ticket from Kingston, Jamaica, instead of from Barbados. The friendly airport attendant looked at the ticket and allowed me to board the plane back to Canada without the proper ticket! I do not think that would happen today.

U of T Stories

African Caribbean Students' Association. Keeping Their Room. Getting It Done.

Shortly after I was hired as a vice president of advancement and external relations at the University of Toronto in 1988, I learned that the elected student association had developed a new policy for student-run clubs on campus. Prior to the policy change, student clubs were given a room of their own to run their activities. Under the new policy, any student club given space on campus was required to open its membership to any student who wanted to join. This was done to ensure inclusivity.

Two student clubs did not agree with that position: the Gay and Lesbian Student Association and the African Caribbean Students' Association (ACSA). Over the next two weeks, the Gay and Lesbian Student Association accepted the new policy, but ACSA did not change its position.

Then one night, the student council changed the locks and put ACSA's equipment, furniture, and files in the hallway. *Not a smart way to resolve a dispute*, I thought. This was, of course, long before social media, but I could see a serious problem beginning for U of T. Two Black community newspapers, *SHARE* and *Contrast*, were developing stories. Of course, U of T's *Varsity* was already running a story.

I was concerned that this problem of no room for ACSA could escalate, and I went to the university president, Dr. George Connell. He heard me out and checked with the legal department, which came back saying the student council had the authority to do what they had done.

Although that was the university's legal position, I remained concerned. I knew several of the students in ACSA — they were smart, tenacious, and creative. A month passed; there were a few more stories in *SHARE* and *Contrast* about what had happened, and the ACSA students were clearly not giving up but were organizing behind the scenes.

One morning I got a call from President Connell. He said, "We have a problem." He told me he had received a call from Mayor Art Eggleton expressing concern about the decision. I was impressed that the students had been able to get through to the mayor. It turns out they had done better than that. They had been in touch with almost every African and Caribbean consulate in Toronto. Toronto was submitting a bid to host the Olympic Games, and clearly Toronto wanted support from Caribbean and African countries (a sizable voting block). Many consuls general had called the mayor's office indicating that if they wanted support for the city's Olympic bid they had better solve the ACSA situation.

President Connell said, "See what you can do to solve this." I went and talked to the students at the ACSA — all they wanted was a room back. I then went to the student council — they understood there was a problem, but they were not going to back down.

I sensed what we needed was a highly credible and trustworthy friend to mediate the situation. I turned to Jean Augustine, a well-respected former school principal, originally from Grenada and, at that time, the chair of the Metropolitan Toronto Housing Authority. (Jean Augustine went on to be a prominent federal member of Parliament and received an honorary doctorate from U of T in 2009.) She agreed on the condition that what she recommended would be implemented.

Jean talked to both sides and, despite her persuasive powers, the student council would not budge. She then looked for a solution within the university. She was familiar with the Transitional Year Programme (TYP) at the university, which took students, often minority students who had dropped out of high school, and fast-tracked them in one year to enter university. The joint coordinators of the programme, Dr. Miriam Rossi and Jack Wayne, came up with a unique solution. They asked the university for an additional classroom, which they would then provide to ACSA. Some of the ACSA students mentored kids in the TYP. There was a big press conference to announce the agreement. The African Caribbean Students' Association was happy, and the university resolved a difficult situation. Representatives from student council did not attend the press conference.

And Toronto placed third in the bid for the Olympics.

Career as Radio Host Ends All Too Soon

While at U of T, I was aware of the student-run radio station that had been in operation since 1966. In 1987, the station received an FM licence from the CRTC and began broadcasting beyond U of T as radio station 98.5 FM, known as CIUT. The station was noncommercial and focused on music, art, and culture.

The university administration felt that CIUT was not providing enough information about exciting activities going on at U of T, such as groundbreaking research and innovative programmes. I was asked to meet with the station manager to discuss this. He listened intently and then suggested that I host a weekly show in prime time, focusing on interesting things happening at the university.

I agreed and, two weeks later, hosted my first show called *U of T Today*.

I invited professors to talk about their work. Some were well known, like Nobel Prize–winner Professor John Polanyi. Others less so, like the Zoology professor who brought in a talking cricket — like really — a talking cricket! That cricket refused to speak — never even made a sound!

I was having the time of my life. I would start the show with my thought of the day. Then I would wind up by taking the words of another broadcaster: "My time is up. Thank you for yours."

Near the end of the term, I went to meet with the station manager to talk about plans for next term. I was bubbling with ideas. He said, rightly, that we needed to get a handle on how the show was doing. He told me that they had no money for research, but in the past, they had listeners call in with feedback. He suggested that in my last show I ask listeners to call in and give feedback. And, as an extra incentive, I would host a dinner at Hart House Grill for the seventh caller.

I made the pitch and waited a couple of weeks to hear from the station manager.

Finally, he called, more than a little embarrassed. I eagerly asked who I was taking to dinner. He responded by saying there would be no dinner as there were only five callers. Two were from my staff. One was from my mother and other from my Aunt Mary. Good old Aunt Mary. One was from a student who said the show was "boring."

And that was that. The show never started up again. My fledgling career as a radio host never got off the ground! The radio station thrives today. And I went back to fundraising.

Fundraising Stories

I have spent much of the last forty years asking people for money for important causes. Asking for money did not come easily to me. At first, I enjoyed talking about the cause but I was uncomfortable asking for money. Wilf Posluns, a leader in the Jewish community, helped me a lot. He said, "Think of it as doing people a favour by asking them to donate. You are giving people a chance to participate in the action. Ask with pride. This is not about begging."

Over the years this became more natural to me. The words of Austin Clarke still resonate: "Listen and Learn." I have learned a lot.

Here are some learnings and stories.

Story 1: Lucille Pratt, the D.L. Pratt Building, and the Piano

Lucille Pratt was a wealthy widow. Her husband, Lorne Pratt, who had passed away in 1969, had a distinguished career in civil engineering at the University of Toronto. His will had specified that, after his wife's passing, a significant sum of money was to go to the Engineering Faculty at the University of Toronto. In the late 1980s, U of T had embarked on its Breakthrough Campaign, and the Engineering Faculty was in desperate need of a new building.

We decided to talk with Mrs. Pratt and her trustees about the idea of flowing the money sooner. We suggested that it would be a way to honour her late husband during her lifetime while still allowing her to maintain her lifestyle. She liked the idea; as she said, "It's my husband's money," and the trustees signed off. Many people worked to make this happen, including the wonderful Malcolm McGrath, the head of Alumni Affairs, who took it upon himself to keep close to Mrs. Pratt.

Keeping close to donors is always important. The gift was $6.2 million — at that time, one of the largest gifts ever made to U of T.

The building is now known as the D.L. Pratt Building, located on King's College Circle. It houses research in electrical engineering and computer science. As we were getting close to the official opening, I talked to Mrs. Pratt about a neat idea of having an electrical robot hand cut the ribbon. She liked that innovative idea. I then asked, and this is always important, "Is there anything special you would like at the opening?" She told me she liked to play the piano; I agreed that playing the piano sounded like a splendid idea. On a lovely spring day in 1991, we opened the building to much fanfare with a robot ribbon cutting and Mrs. Pratt playing the piano.

The following day, there was a major story in the news about the opening and a lovely picture of Mrs. Pratt, detailing her remarkable contribution honouring her late husband. I called her up. She said she had never had her picture in the paper before. She said several friends had called her up, complimenting her. She added, though, that she had a problem. She told me her gardener of some twenty-five years had come up to her and said, "Mrs. Pratt, I never knew you were so rich. I want a raise!" The gardener got his raise!

Mrs. Pratt continued to play the piano and maintained a wonderful lifestyle. She often came back to the university and toured the building named after her husband. Malcolm McGrath continued to visit her. When she passed away in 2005, she gave her entire estate to charity.

Story 2: Helen Gardiner Phelan and Wayne and Shuster

Helen Gardiner was a philanthropist and impressive community volunteer. Her husband, Paul Phelan, built Cara Foods into an iconic Canadian brand. She had chaired the boards of both Women's College Hospital and Lyndhurst Hospital. Her great love was U of T's University College, where she had been a student in the 1940s. She had also briefly been an actress and enjoyed being in the University College Follies, a student theatre group that has a proud history going back to 1880.

Knowing Helen was a longtime supporter of the university, we approached her in 1989 during the early days of our Breakthrough Campaign. She immediately responded with a gift of $100,000. Though significant, it was not a breakthrough gift.

In those days, we had a Campaign Advisory Committee consisting of friends of the university, many of whom were well connected. Two people who served on that committee were U of T grads and, at that time, Canada's most famous and successful comedians, Johnny Wayne and Frank Shuster. We talked with them about how we might achieve bigger gifts and gave Helen Gardiner as an example.

Immediately Johnny Wayne said, "We know Helen, she was in the UC follies with us back in the 1940s." Frank Shuster piped in with the fact that the UC Playhouse needed a major renovation at a cost of $1 million. The idea was born that Wayne and Shuster would visit their old friend Helen Gardiner Phelan, who they had not seen in many years, and talk fondly about the UC Playhouse.

Two days later, I received a call from Helen withdrawing her $100,000 gift and replacing it with a $1 million gift to renovate the playhouse. When an additional $200,000 was needed for air conditioning and other renovations, Helen provided the funds.

The grand opening of the Helen Gardiner Phelan Playhouse was a huge success. One of my staff found a picture of Helen with Wayne and Shuster from the UC Follies back in the 1940s. We blew it up six feet high and gave it to Helen. She put it proudly in her Forest Hill home and then said the magic words — and these are always the magic words — "There is more money to come."

Story 3: Peter Bronfman — Rooting for the Underdog

I got to know Peter Bronfman well after he moved to Toronto from Montreal. I liked him a lot.

He and his brother, Edward, formed the very successful Edper Investments (now Brookfield) and hired great people to run it.

Peter spent a great deal of his time doing what he loved, helping people on the margins succeed. He focused on the less high-profile causes. For example, he spent time at Nellie's, a women's shelter, and St. Stephen's House, a neighbourhood settlement house.

He also encouraged senior staff in the Edper organization to get involved with charity work and was pleased when they did so. He joined the board of the United Way when I was there, and we would talk from time to time about how to create a caring and civil society.

When I left the United Way to work at the University of Toronto, he was not at all happy with me. He thought I was leaving the grassroots and going to the ivory tower. Nevertheless, he did donate $100,000 to U of T, I think to personally support me. I knew that Peter could give far more. But for Peter, the cause was everything. So I did what a fundraiser should never do … I sent the money back! I thanked him, of course, and said there would come a time when I would find a project at the university that he would be proud to support.

A year later, I was made aware of a major renovation being planned for Woodsworth College on St. George Street. This is the college for part-time students. Several of the students came from difficult circumstances, and many were not young. I met with four single mothers who were receiving social assistance, who had made the courageous decision to head back to university. I thought this would be a good fit for Peter.

I called him up and suggested he visit Woodsworth College and have lunch with these four women. He said, "Gordon, you are setting me up." I told him he was absolutely right! Peter did have lunch with these women. He liked what he heard. He got to know them personally, and he paid for the renovation of Woodsworth. Peter was never big on personal recognition. This made him an anomaly in today's world, where almost every building has someone's name on it. Peter behaved in the historic tradition of Jewish philanthropy whereby getting it done is more important than recognition.

As Woodsworth's grand opening got closer, I asked Peter what we could do to thank him. He said, "Plant a tree and don't put a plaque on it." At the opening, I stood next to Peter — I could tell he was pleased. He liked being in the background and seeing it just happen.

After Peter died in 1996, his company made a major donation to Woodsworth College. Today, more than twenty-five years after his death, Peter's widow, Lynda Hamilton, is still involved with and supports Woodsworth.

Story 4: Jack Cockwell, Brookfield Corporation, and the Legacy of Peter Bronfman

I have known Jack Cockwell for over forty years. He is one of Canada's most successful business leaders. In the last fifteen years, he has also become a leading philanthropist — I believe, giving well over $200 million dollars to a variety of causes. Jack is very humble and rarely talks publicly about his giving.

The question always is, why do people do what they do?

For Jack Cockwell and other senior leaders at Brookfield, it goes back to the legacy of Peter Bronfman. He believed deeply that, if an individual does well, then that individual has a responsibility to get involved with and support the community.

Brookfield has done exceedingly well over the years. The senior leadership of that company has been involved (as volunteers and major donors) in almost every major charity, including the United Way, YMCA, Ryerson University (now Toronto Metropolitan

University), the Royal Ontario Museum, St. Michael's Hospital, Trails Youth Initiatives, and many more.

I have watched Jack Cockwell's giving over the years, and I have been involved in a few of his gifts. I believe his motives are as follows:

He wants to honour the legacy that Peter Bronfman began.

He wants to honour the company that he helped build and that provided him with the income to make large donations.

He supports causes that he believes in deeply and that are led by strong, competent, and inspirational leaders.

He is not big on having his name attached to his donations; rather, he has chosen on several occasions to honour his mother.

A couple of years ago, he gave $10 million to name George Brown College's signature tall wood building, Limberlost Place. This name connects with the family's involvement with Limberlost Forest and Wildlife Reserve and their commitment to sustainable forestry.

Peter's legacy continues. Jack Cockwell and his colleagues have learned the lesson well. They are honouring Peter's legacy through their actions. The next generation of leaders at Brookfield is taking note.

Story 5: George and Sheila Connell and Lalaine de Vera

George Connell was the president of the University of Toronto who recruited me. We also lived on the same street for many years. We became good friends. When my wife and I went off for three years to build the first-ever YMCA in Tobago, George and his wife, Sheila, were early supporters.

By the time we returned from Tobago in 2011, George was in the early stages of Alzheimer's. His health was deteriorating, and it became difficult for Sheila to continue to care for him at home. He soon moved into the Revera facility on Spadina Road, where I would visit him every couple of weeks. We would often have fun travelling down memory lane together. He told me about growing up in Prince

Albert, Saskatchewan, where his father had been John Diefenbaker's dentist, and that is how he became a Conservative.

I would talk with Sheila from time to time, and learned that George's health needs were such that he needed to move to a long-term care facility. Sheila had heard good things about Kensington Gardens. My mother-in-law, Joan Campbell, had lived there for several years and we loved the place. Sheila applied to the local Community Care Access Centre (CCAC), and George was put on a waiting list. It took time, but eventually George was admitted to Kensington. Sheila, I think, believes to this day I had something to do with this. I kept telling her I did not. There is no queue jumping with the CCAC.

George settled in quite nicely at Kensington. My younger brother, Jim, who has lived courageously with schizophrenia since his early twenties, was a volunteer in the Tuck Shop at Kensington, and he would often see and chat with George. I also continued to visit. Sheila was always there for her George.

At one point, Sheila called and said she wanted to donate to George Brown College, where I was on contract, in appreciation for the time I was spending with George. I was grateful for this gesture and thought the donation would be about $200. I was amazed when a cheque arrived for $10,000! I called Sheila and thanked her. I indicated that it might be appropriate to name a room down at the new Health Sciences Waterfront Campus after her and George. She said she would think about it and get back to me. She did call back and said, "George and I do not need that. Why not name it after a real caregiver? They are the people who treat George with dignity."

I came home and chatted with my wife. We had a brilliant idea. We made a personal donation and contacted others, raising $50,000. We then asked that George Brown honour Lalaine de Vera. Lalaine is a personal support worker who helped raise our boys and then looked after both our mothers. She was born and raised in the Philippines, worked under difficult conditions as a caregiver in Singapore, and came to Canada in her twenties.

We chatted with the head of the Personal Support Worker Programme at George Brown College about this idea. She loved it.

Many of the students in the programme come from the Philippines. We approached Lalaine, who at first hesitated and said she did not deserve this. Finally, after some persuading, she agreed.

On a cold January day in 2013, something quite magical happened at the Waterfront Campus as the Lalaine de Vera Room was officially named. The room is a replica apartment used for hands-on training of Personal Support Worker students. Lalaine's family was there, as well as students in the programme. George Brown President Anne Sado made a speech, as did Chancellor Sally Horsfall Eaton. Then Lalaine got up, thanked everybody, and said that caring for people is what she loves to do. Sheila Connell, my wife and I, our boys, and my brother Jim all looked on and realized we were part of honouring a great woman.

The media got it too. There was a mention in the Filipino press, the CBC did a story, and Carol Goar of the *Toronto Star* wrote an article titled "New Twist on Philanthropy."

I continued to visit George Connell at Kensington Gardens until his death in 2015. Even though he no longer seemed to know me, I always felt the better for going. And it strikes me that, by honouring her husband this way, Sheila Connell did a magnificent thing. I sense, knowing George as I did, that he would have been pleased.

From left to right: Sheila Connell, Lalaine de Vera,
Jim Cressy, Joanne Campbell, Gordon Cressy.

Story 6: The CAW and the Chair in Social Justice Studies

In my early days at Ryerson, I learned that the Canadian Auto Workers Union (CAW) was looking to establish the first union-funded university chair. It would be in Social Justice Studies and would honour the highly regarded and, at times, fiery union leader Sam Guindon, who was retiring from the CAW. Many universities wanted this chair. The CAW set up a unique process whereby each university interested would be interviewed by a three-person panel set up by the CAW. The members of the panel were Bob White, a past president of the CAW; Rosemary Brown, Jamaican born and the first Black person elected as an MPP; and Carol Phillips, executive assistant to Buzz Hargrove (president of the CAW).

We learned that eleven universities were in the running. Ryerson, though, had prided itself for many years on being the grassroots university in downtown Toronto.

As we were discussing our presentation, one of the student leaders advised us to just be ourselves. Nothing fancy, but have our people tell our story. So off we went without our president. We gave each of our representatives one minute to make our pitch. What a pitch they made! The head of the student council, the head of the Canadian Union of Public Employees, the head of the Ontario Public Service Employees Union, and the head of the Ryerson Faculty Association. I basically just showed up and watched.

In the end, I was told on the quiet that our approach had sealed the deal.

When the decision was announced, the press said that the CAW had awarded the Sam Guindon chair in Social Justice to Ryerson the "working-class university." President Claude Lajeunesse was not happy with that headline. Many of us, though, knew the significance of that headline. Sam Guindon was thrilled.

A few years later, when Nelson Mandela and his wife received joint honorary degrees from Ryerson, the same principle was at play. But that is another story.

Story 7: Michael Adams and the Art of Listening

I was out one night at a cocktail party and I started to chat with Michael Adams, who had become well known for his work as the head of Environics Research and as an emerging writer. We knew each other a little bit from political days and we were basically catching up.

I told him that I had moved on from the United Way to the University of Toronto, and was now responsible for leading the Breakthrough fundraising campaign.

He told me he might be interested in creating a chair in Polish Studies. I was amazed because I had no idea that Michael had a Polish background. Our conversation drifted to other topics, but I filed that idea in my head.

On Monday when I got into work, I called a U of T colleague who specialized in languages and told him to get in touch with Michael Adams to pursue this discussion of Polish studies.

The next day, he called me back to say he had an embarrassing conversation with Michael Adams. He told me that Michael certainly remembered my conversation with him. However, he was clear that he said, "polling studies" not "Polish studies." Embarrassed, yes, but daunted — no! I immediately called our Political Science Department and told them to get in touch with Michael Adams.

It is critical to listen to and honour donors' wishes.

Story 8: Opportunity House and Warren Seyffert — There Is No Free Lunch

Back when I worked at Opportunity House, Warren Seyffert was the chair of our board. At an even earlier time, we had served together on a small nonprofit board dealing with young people and drug abuse. He was a lawyer with the firm Lang Michener.

We needed to raise some money for Opportunity House. To be frank, we were dirt poor and knew little about fundraising. We could not afford a brochure or anything fancy. Warren, however, had several friends with money. And those friends had friends. Warren's idea made good sense. Rather than tell people about the work of our group home, far better to have people come and see it and meet the boys who were living there.

People were busy and it was difficult to schedule visits. We then had a very cool idea. At 11:45 a.m., we would pick up Warren's friends in our Opportunity House van and drive to the house on Bowden Street for lunch with our boys. We would then get them back downtown before 2:00 p.m.

For the kids, it would be a chance to meet with adults who were doing quite well. Warren's friends would see firsthand what a group home was all about. And Warren would have a chance to share with his friends a programme that was important to him.

It worked big-time. After people got back to work, Warren called his friends and asked for a donation. They all donated. A couple got involved as volunteers. For our boys, it improved their communication skills and their self-confidence too.

When people can see it and feel it, they are more likely to support it.

Story 9: Albert Reichman — Listen to the Quiet and Do Not Babble

The Reichmann family owned Olympia and York, the major development company. They built First Canadian Place and were involved in developments around the world. They had a well-deserved reputation of being very generous to Jewish causes, but they had not been involved with the United Way.

One of our volunteers, Michael Cornelissen, then president of Royal Trust, had come to know Albert Reichmann through his involvement with the Brascan Group. Michael arranged for us to meet. Our usual plan was to prepare a fifteen-minute meeting, five minutes for presentation and ten minutes for discussion.

If it went longer, so be it — but it was not to be our initiative.

We stuck to plan, and after Michael introduced me, I made our pitch, talking about the importance of the United Way to the whole community. I suggested that, as leaders in Toronto, it would be important for the Reichmann family to be involved with the United Way.

My job was done. I was finished. Albert looked at me. I looked at him.

We looked at each other for what seemed a very, very long time. I was getting quite uncomfortable. But I realized deep down that I had said what needed to be said, and there was no point in saying anything more. Finally, after what seemed like thirty minutes (it was probably only forty-five seconds), he looked at Michael and me and simply said, "Good presentation." He asked a couple of questions and then we were out of there. He did make a large donation.

Story 10: Live Auctions

I have been doing charity auctions now for over thirty years. It all started one evening at a Chinese restaurant on Dundas Street. I was attending a fundraising banquet for University Settlement House. (Over the years, I have attended many banquets at that restaurant.) They were having a live auction and it was going very badly. I was watching it closely and made the mistake of saying a little too loudly, "I can do better than that!" Next thing I knew, I was up on stage conducting the auction!

Since then, I have done big auctions, auctioning off condominiums and high-end automobiles; and small ones in Regent Park where the top item was a toaster oven. Mind you, the homemade rum punch got a lot of bids!

Most auctions go very well and are a lot of fun. Sometimes though, the items do not match the donors. I will never forget the auction for Sick Kids when all the items were one-of-a-kind designer dresses … all size two! There were virtually no bidders!

I have done the Dragon Ball auction for over twenty years to raise money for the Yee Hong Centres for Geriatric Care. In some years, we auctioned off a condo offered by Tridel and several very high-end automobiles.

My son, Joe, has joined me as a co-auctioneer from time to time.

One that has been great fun is the annual University of the West Indies (UWI) fundraiser, which takes place in Toronto and provides scholarships for UWI students at its three campuses in the Caribbean. I have been part of it every year since it started in 2010.

Actually, my wife and I were working in Tobago with the YMCA when I got a call about doing the auction for the first UWI gala. I naturally said yes as I assumed it would be in Port of Spain, Trinidad, just a twenty-minute flight from Tobago.

Imagine my surprise when I got a call a week before the event to learn it was in Toronto! Not sure how it all happened, but I am certain my incredibly generous friend Ray Chang booked a ticket for me. I flew up to Toronto on the Saturday, did the auction on the Saturday night, and flew back to Tobago on the Sunday morning.

I have auctioned off many different items over the years — but at the UWI event, things moved to a different level entirely.

One year, we auctioned the running shoes worn by Usain Bolt, Yohan Blake, and Warren Weir, who had won gold, silver, and bronze medals, respectively, in the 200-metre event at the 2012 Olympics. We raised over $20,000!

Another year, the enormously popular Shaggy (Orville Richard Burrell), a UWI award winner, agreed to perform a couple of songs if people would donate. Ray Chang and Michael Lee-Chin started the bidding; others joined in, and before we knew it, we had raised $33,000. Shaggy brought the house down with two of his great songs, "Angel" and "Boombastic."

The key in auctions is to make them entertaining and to move the bidding along quickly. Experience has taught me that something that drags on too long becomes a drag.

The Dragon Ball auction with my son Joe.

The Montreal Massacre

On December 6, 1989, fourteen young women were murdered at École Polytechnique in Montreal. Canadians were in shock.

A memorial service was planned at the university. Speakers were organized. I was invited to speak — I was the only male speaker.

I reflected on this for some time and realized that men should prepare to confront other men when needed. For years, I had quietly tolerated sexist and racist jokes from people I knew. Now I decided just being silent was not enough. I said something about this in my remarks at the memorial service. I don't remember much else of what I said.

What I do remember, though, was the speech given by Dr. Ursula Franklin, esteemed professor in the Faculty of Applied Science and Engineering at the University of Toronto. Besides being a brilliant engineer in a field dominated by men, she was strong and outspoken on many of the issues of the day. I remember there was some concern about what she might say, but she had earned the right to speak — and speak she did. Hers was not a soothing voice but a plaintive cry that shook Convocation Hall.

She said this:

In remembrance, what is it that we are called to reflect? We remember the fourteen students in Montreal. But we also remember that they were abandoned. Our memory should not block out the fact that Marc Lépine, at one of his killing stations, went into a classroom in which there were men and women. He asked them to separate into two groups and when this did not happen, he fired a shot to the ceiling. Then it did happen. The men left. Fourteen women were killed and Marc Lépine could leave this classroom. It is not as much a question of how he got in, but it is a question of how he got out. In our memory and reflection, we have to include that these women were abandoned by their fellow students.

Not long after, Jack Layton and others created the White Ribbon Campaign, which is crucial in today's world. The purpose of this campaign is outlined on Wikipedia:

> The **White Ribbon Campaign** (**WRC**) is a global movement of men and boys working to end male violence against women and girls. It was formed by a group of pro-feminist men in London, Ontario, in November 1991 as a response to the École Polytechnique massacre of female students by Marc Lépine in 1989. The campaign was intended to raise awareness about the prevalence of male violence against women, with the ribbon symbolizing "the idea of men giving up their arms." Active in over 60 countries, the movement seeks to promote healthy relationships, gender equity, and a compassionate vision of masculinity.

I started, in my small way, to tell people that sexist and racist jokes were not okay. It began when my dad and I were playing in the annual Member-Guest Golf Tournament at the Toronto Hunt Club. We had a great day and joined everyone for dinner and trophy presentations.

The master of ceremonies started his remarks with a series of inappropriate jokes. I sensed some of the members were upset, but most laughed right along. I then looked at the female staff serving the meal. Some of them had worked at the club for over twenty years. I could tell by their body language that they did not find this funny, and I wondered what they told their families about how the members of this elite golf course behaved.

I did not take the emcee on in public — but I did in private. He listened politely enough. The next year, my dad and I were back. It was the same emcee.

He started by saying that some yahoo last year was a party pooper, complaining about the jokes. And off he went again. The crowd did not laugh so loud. I turned to my father and said, "Dad, we are leaving." And we did. The next year that emcee was gone and the jokes stopped.

One of my senior volunteers used to email out sexist and racist jokes. I am sure he must have thought them funny. I just deleted them without opening them. However, one Friday afternoon, I opened his latest joke. It was awful. I wrote him and said it was inappropriate and wondered what his wife and daughter or the female members of our board would think if they received these jokes.

He did not write back and our friendship diminished greatly. Sometimes you just do what you must do.

The Learning Partnership

In the fall of 1993, I was appointed the founding president of what was then called the Metropolitan Toronto Learning Partnership (later we changed the name to The Learning Partnership).

The idea was to bring together leaders from education, business, and the community to restore confidence in public education by developing programmes and activities championing our education system. This focus resonated with me strongly, as I believe deeply that, if we do not get it right with our young people in their early days, it will be impossible when they are older.

My mother was shocked that I would leave a "prestigious position as vice president of the University of Toronto" to head this fledgling Learning Partnership with no staff and virtually no money! Fortunately, John Black Aird thought this was an important new initiative, and he convinced my parents that I was doing the right thing.

Before applying for the job, I was on holiday with my wife and two sons, Joseph and Keith, in Myrtle Beach. I was watching television one evening and saw a report about a new event called Take Your Daughters to Work. The idea was that fathers or mothers would take their Grade 9 daughters to their place of work for a day. The intent was to build self-esteem in young women and show them the possibilities in the workplace. The added benefit was that it would give them the chance to see what their parents did at work.

Shortly after I started at The Learning Partnership, I went to New York to visit the Ms. Foundation for Women, the founders of Take Your Daughters to Work, and came away excited by this initiative.

I discussed this idea with some teachers, business people, and labour leaders. All liked the idea, but we all thought that the programme should be expanded to include boys and girls. Lori Cranson, our newly hired programme director, said we could work with teachers to develop a curriculum that would help prepare young people for the day.

The question now was what to call this programme. It seemed wordy to call the programme Take Our Daughters and Sons to Work Day. (That is what it is now called in the United States.) We first thought of using the word *youth*. That year, the well-loved movie *My Cousin Vinny* had come out. I remember the judge in the film saying in a sarcastic voice, "What's a youth?" He was right. We then came to the word *kid*. So, in November 1994, we started Take Our Kids to Work Day in Toronto.

It took off. Kids loved it because they got to see their parents in a whole new light. Parents got a chance to show their kids exactly what they did. I think that the parents also came to appreciate how difficult the job of a teacher is! The media loved it, and members of the media invited their kids to anchor the reporting on Take Our Kids to Work Day, so the kids told the story. Scotiabank, a founding sponsor of the programme, agreed to take kids who did not have parents in the workplace. Many companies also agreed.

Not everything went according to plan. At one workplace, a kid found a free pop machine on the executive floor, took two cases of Coke, and sold them in the lobby over the noon hour. The executive wasn't sure whether to report him or hire him, as he admired the entrepreneurial spirit!

In 1995, Take Our Kids to Work went across Ontario, and the following year across Canada. Every year, on the first Wednesday of November, 250,000 students participate in over 75,000 workplaces right across the country. It became the flagship programme of The Learning Partnership. It has since started many other initiatives, such as the Entrepreneur Adventure Programme and Invention Convention, programmes which are now also Canada-wide, but there remains to this day a branding issue … Take Our Kids to Work is better known across Canada than The Learning Partnership!

Sadly, The Learning Partnership could not sustain its funding during the pandemic and closed in 2022, but Take our Kids to Work continues.

Nelson Mandela Visits Toronto

"It always seems impossible until it's done."

Nelson Mandela made three visits to Canada during his lifetime. I was privileged to have a front-row seat for two of them.

If It Is the Right Thing to Do, Find a Way to Do It

In the spring of 1998, I got a call from my best friend, John Piper. We had worked closely together on the Bishop Desmund Tutu visit back in 1986, and he was aware that Nelson Mandela had been invited by Prime Minister Jean Chrétien for a state visit to Ottawa.

Zeib Jeeva, a longtime activist with the African Nation Congress in Toronto, suggested inviting Mandela to come to Toronto after Ottawa to launch the Nelson Mandela Children's Fund in Canada. He talked with Billy Modise, the South African high commissioner to Canada, who liked the idea — as long as Zeib and John could guarantee a successful launch.

This was to be no ordinary event. When John Piper thinks big, he thinks huge. John had the idea of schoolchildren, thousands and thousands of them, coming to hear Nelson Mandela speak. He said the South African government was supportive of this idea, and he wanted to know if The Learning Partnership was willing to provide staff support for such an event.

The idea was to have Mandela come to Toronto near the end of September and speak to 45,000 students. It was now May. John made a presentation to our board and basically said we had two weeks to sign on, as the time was already very tight.

Our board was intrigued but rightly cautious. This idea, while compelling, did not really fit our mandate. We had no facility, no funding, and no support from anyone. Board member Harold Brathwaite (the first Black director of education in Ontario, with the Peel Board of Education) said he would check out the teachers' federations and gauge their support. I said I would check out potential donors, and others on the board said that they would check the idea out with their various networks.

When we gathered again, the update was not encouraging. At the time, the teachers' federations were on "work to rule" due to ongoing battles with Ontario Premier Mike Harris and his Conservative government. Meanwhile I had not raised a dime. Early conversations with the owners of the SkyDome revealed lukewarm interest at best.

We all looked at each other and said, "Let's do it!" The data did not justify that decision, but the idea of President Nelson Mandela coming to Toronto and speaking to 45,000 students was just too compelling.

We all moved into high gear. John Piper took almost three months off to volunteer full time. John Honderich of the *Toronto Star* signed on immediately to be the media sponsor. Buzz Hargrove, the president of the Canadian Auto Workers Union, said, "Count us in for a $75,000 donation." The CAW had a long history of supporting the anti-apartheid struggle. He also said, "Leave the teachers' federations to me." Two days later, the teachers' federations were in.

Over the summer, things started to come together quickly. The federal and provincial governments joined in with donations. Prime

Minister Jean Chrétien agreed to attend. The Royal Bank joined in and other companies did too.

The SkyDome (now the Rogers Centre) offered their facility at a cut-rate cost. Entertainers agreed to perform free of charge. Things were coming together.

As September arrived and schools were back in session, Lloyd McKell, who had worked with teachers over the summer to develop a school curriculum for the visit, took charge of coordinating transit for kids across the Greater Toronto area. As part of their gift, the federal government wanted students from across Canada to attend. Air Canada was about to go on strike. Canadian Airlines said with an Air Canada strike, they would be too busy to offer spaces on planes. My old high school friend Carl Dickinson worked for Canadian Holidays Limited. He discussed the idea with the president, Errol Francis, who was originally from Uganda. Nelson Mandela was his hero. He simply said, "Do it," and Canadian Holidays became our airline sponsor, bringing kids from across the country. Carl and Errol made sure students from every province in Canada would attend the event. People in Toronto volunteered to put the kids up free of charge.

Robin Benger, originally from South Africa and an accomplished documentary film maker, convinced the CBC to cover the event live across Canada. Schools were being encouraged to have classes watch the event on television. The world's largest classroom was rapidly taking shape.

Robert and Brenda Rooney, two social-justice activists and brilliant event organizers, volunteered their time to produce the show. By then we simply called what was about to happen "Mandela and the Children."

The day before the event, kids from Toronto-area schools were practising as a huge choir at the SkyDome. I took a taxi back to our office and got to chatting with the Somali taxi driver. He told me how excited he was about Mandela's visit and how he and his wife and three kids would love to attend, but that there were no tickets available. That morning we were organizing the seating for the VIP guests. I made an instant decision that my new Somali friend was a

VIP guest. I told him to wait, and I went up to the office and came down with five tickets for seats in the second row, which I gave to him. I think Nelson Mandela would have approved.

Lloyd McKell was front and centre, seeing that everyone got to the SkyDome on time. On the morning of September 28, my wife and I and our two young sons arrived early. We watched as the SkyDome filled up.

The Canadian government had originally wanted Prime Minister Chrétien to accompany Nelson Mandela on the golf cart as he entered the SkyDome. The South African government wanted just Mandela on his own. Over the summer, Nelson Mandela had married Graça Machel, and so it was decided that the newly married couple should arrive together. Problem averted. Nelson Mandela and Graça Machel entered the SkyDome to a spontaneous outpouring of love and affection. The atmosphere was electric. Nelson Mandela, then age eighty, literally danced on stage. The musicians were magnificent, with a mixture of African, hip-hop, and Indigenous music. The dancers danced, and Nelson and Graça swayed along with them. The politicians, who usually speak too long, did not. They knew this was Mandela's moment.

Then it was Nelson Mandela's turn. The thunderous standing ovation went on and on. Then it went quiet as he began to speak. He told us of his love of children and how, during his twenty-seven years in prison, he was not ever able to hold or see a child. He talked of his love of Canada and the important role Canadians had played in the fight against apartheid.

He challenged us all to help build a better world. Nelson Mandela and his wife left to an extraordinary outpouring of love, affection, and applause. We were laughing and crying at the same time. He had inspired us all. We lingered longer than necessary, but we wanted the moment to last forever. Students who attended the event wrote about their experience. The amazing Lloyd McKell organized some of the young people's stories into book form. The back page of the book is copied here, including a quote from my young son Keith.

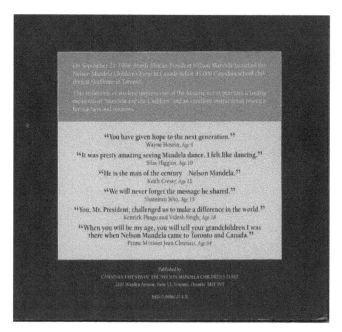

Occasionally I meet someone who attended the event. They remember it well.

Looking back, I am grateful that John Piper, Zeib Jeeva, Lloyd McKell, and others asked The Learning Partnership to sign on. Was it the right thing to do? Absolutely.

Nelson Mandela and Graça Machel come to Ryerson

In early 2001, several ideas began to gain traction about bringing Nelson Mandela to Canada for a third visit. By that time, I had become the vice president of advancement at Ryerson University.

Debbie Chant, a longtime Ryerson senior staff member, had proposed that we give an honorary doctorate to Graça Machel, now married to Nelson Mandela. Graça Machel was a powerhouse in her own right — a politician, human rights and children's advocate, and respected leader in her native Mozambique. She had also been married to the president of Mozambique, Samora Machel, who was tragically killed when his plane was shot down by the apartheid regime. A formal request had been made to have her visit and receive an honorary degree, but no word had come back.

Debbie knew of my work with the Nelson Mandela Children's Fund and made the splendid suggestion that we consider joint honorary doctorates for both Graça Machel and Nelson Mandela. I got in touch with Bongi Mkhabela, the head of the Nelson Mandela Children's Fund in South Africa, and Pat Van der Merwe, who worked directly for Mr. Mandela. They both liked the idea but also thought we should look at fundraising as part of this idea.

Stephen Lewis, the former Ontario politician and United Nations Special Envoy for HIV and Aids in Africa, was a close friend of both Nelson Mandela and Graça Machel. For many years, Graça Machel has served as chair of the African Advisory Board of the quite extraordinary Stephen Lewis Foundation. Stephen had for many years served as a distinguished visiting faculty member at Ryerson. Many Canadian universities were, of course, clamouring to give Nelson Mandela an honorary degree. My view is that the final decision came down to this: first, an encouraging call to Nelson and Graça from their dear friend Stephen Lewis, extolling the virtues of Ryerson; and second, the idea of granting the honorary doctorate to both Graça and Nelson.

At the same time, the Canadian government was looking at making Nelson Mandela an honorary Canadian citizen. Stephen LeDrew, then president of the Liberal Party of Canada, got involved. So did Ray Heard, a South African by birth, a longtime Liberal, and chief of staff to former Prime Minister John Turner. Ray's brother was a senior official in the South African government, and Ray had the added advantage of being close to wealthy Toronto philanthropists Gerry Schwartz and Heather Reisman. He suggested that they might host a reception to raise money for the Nelson Mandela Children's Fund.

In addition, Lloyd McKell, Zeib Jeeva, Bahadur Madhani (then chair of the Nelson Mandela Children's Fund), John Piper, and others thought that if Nelson Mandela and Graça Machel were coming to Toronto it would be great to name a public school after Nelson Mandela. Discussion began with Park Public School, on the edge of Regent Park. Parents and children were thrilled with the idea, but at the same time, they did not want to lose the history of Park Public School. A recommendation that produced smiles all around was to call it Nelson Mandela Park Public School.

Soon all parts came together. The school opening was set for Saturday, November 17, at 9:30 a.m. The Ryerson honorary doctorate celebrations would start at 11:00 a.m. The fundraising event was an early evening reception at the home of Gerry Schwartz and Heather Reisman, costing $5,000 per couple. The Mandelas were staying at the Four Seasons Hotel for free, courtesy of Issy Sharp. They were to leave on the Sunday for Ottawa, and on Monday, November 19, Nelson Mandela was to be the first living person to receive honorary Canadian citizenship.

The picture above was taken when Nelson Mandela arrived at the Four Seasons Hotel. It looks like I am greeting Nelson Mandela. In truth, world-famous singer Tony Bennett was there to greet Nelson Mandela. The photographer was badly positioned and could get only the back of Tony Bennett's head in the picture.

The opening at Nelson Mandela Park Public School was perfect. There was a brief magical moment when the young girl making a presentation to Nelson Mandela started to cry. Mandela stopped and wiped the tears from her eyes and gave her a hug. That picture went viral around the world.

His brief speech is copied here from the Toronto District School Board.

Nelson Mandela's Speech — November 17, 2001

Ladies and gentleman, and young people, who are here, my wife, Graça Machel and myself, are greatly honoured to be here this morning, and to meet all of you. We know that you are the future leaders, not only of Toronto, not only of Canada, but of the entire world. When you are old, many of you are going to be members of Parliament, you are going to be ambassadors and represent your country in foreign lands, you are going to be members of the cabinet, you are going to be Prime Ministers! You are the future leaders of the world, and it is an honour for us to be here to interact with you.

Both my wife and I were once as young as you are. When we see you, we think of those beautiful days when we had no problems, when we played the whole day whenever we had opportunities. We were here in 1998, it was one of the most of unforgettable occasions, because we met thousands of children who inspired us a great deal. We now know there are children all over the world as young as you are, that these children in other countries are very poor and need help, and we are pleased to know that the children of this school have identified themselves with the children of South Africa and have raised funds and continue to raise funds in order to help our children. When you do that, you help those children not only to be able to go to school, to buy books, but even to help them feed themselves, but to inspire them. You make them feel that they are not alone.

Toronto is a place where you have our Children's Fund and where various people have contributed generously to make sure that this fund has sufficient resources to tackle questions of poverty, of disease, of HIV, which is a wiping out large populations. That amount of money that you have raised is going to encourage children elsewhere to do the same thing to help the children of South Africa who are very poor. Now we are here today to launch your new school name, and it is a great privilege for me and my wife to do so.

In the meantime, I want you to know I love each and every one of you not as my children, not even as my grandchildren, but as my great-grandchildren. I have 29 grandchildren and I have 6 great-grandchildren. You are younger than my great-grandchildren, but I love you from the bottom of my heart. My wife and I will not forget the beautiful and innocent faces that we are looking at now. Thank you very much.

Then followed the honorary doctorate presentations at Ryerson. Suhana Meharchand, a native of South Africa, a Ryerson graduate, and a well-known CBC journalist, was the emcee. At the start, she could not help herself. She said to Nelson Mandela, "I've always wanted to hug you," and she went across stage and did hug him! The CBC carried it all. The music by Molly Johnson was electrifying. Children's singer Raffi led his choir in singing "Turn This World Around." We all joined in, singing and clapping together.

We then listened intently to moving speeches by Graça Machel and Nelson Mandela. Mandela's humility shone through when he said he was touched that he could attend an event honouring his high-profile wife. I sat with my family and savoured the moment, realizing that Mandela would probably never return to Canada again.

That evening I sensed the Mandelas were tired after a long day. The Toronto elites showed up at the home of Gerry Schwartz and Heather Reisman. Even movie stars Michael Douglas and Catharine Zeta-Jones were there.

The idea was that, in return for their $5,000 contribution, each couple would have their picture taken with Nelson Mandela. It all started to go very wrong when the photographer took the first photo and the fuse blew. Mandela looked none too happy. He had eye problems dating back to his prison days on Robben Island, digging limestone, and the bright lights were bothering him. His personal assistant, Zelda La Grange, took charge fast.

Zelda loved Mandela and was very protective of him, especially when people wanted too much of him. After all, he was eighty-three at the time. After the fuse blew a second time, Zelda turned to John Piper, who was organizing the pictures, and said very clearly, "No more pictures."

John tried his best to organize group pictures. Zelda was having none of it. She said more sternly than the first time, "No more pictures or we are leaving!" She meant it, and no more photos were taken.

Mandela then spoke to us all about the role Canada had played in the apartheid struggle and how South Africa was, as a new democracy, going through growing pains.

Eventually, it was time to go home. People left the better for seeing the Mandelas, but without the promised pictures. Shortly thereafter, Gerry and Heather renovated their house and upgraded the wiring!

We all went to Ottawa for the honorary citizenship presentation. I invited my wife's uncle, Ross Campbell, a career diplomat who had thought Black liberation in South Africa would never happen in his lifetime.

Then it was over. The Ryerson student newspaper interviewed me. They mentioned that people said I had played a key role in the event. I had learned by then that humility is the best way to respond, so I said just tell them that Gordon Cressy was a bit player in the event. Unfortunately, the article came out saying Gordon Cressy says he was a "big" player in the event. One letter can make a huge difference. The *Ryersonian* editor apologized at some length and put a retraction in the next issue. No one saw it.

Canadian Tire and Starting Jump Start

Get the Inside Onside — Before You Go Outside

It was the spring of 2002, and I was sitting at a luncheon chatting with Martha Billes, chair of Canadian Tire, after she had received an honorary doctorate from Ryerson University. I did not know a lot about Canadian Tire except that I sure shopped there and I liked the idea that a Canadian company was competing successfully with American invaders like Walmart and Home Depot.

She asked about my plans. I indicated that I was happy working at Ryerson but, every five years or so, I liked to have a new challenge. We got along well, and she suggested that I might want to explore Canadian Tire. She went on to mention that a senior position was opening that might interest me. I was both excited about this new opportunity and skeptical about my ability to adapt to the private sector.

Not long after that lunch, I got a call from Wayne Sales, the president of Canadian Tire, asking me to meet with him. We hit it off immediately. He described the job of vice president of communications, which, among other things, oversaw the company's charitable arm, the Canadian Tire Foundation for Families.

Next thing, I was meeting one on one with the senior executives of Canadian Tire. I was impressed with their knowledge and pride in the company. Things were going quite well, and I was asked to meet with the senior vice president of finance. He asked me a couple of questions, and I quickly realized that I was completely out of my depth! When he asked me my position on derivatives, I knew I was done. The only answer I could come up with was to mumble something about my father being a banker! A few weeks later Wayne Sales called and asked me for dinner.

He said I had a lot to offer and that, although the VP communications position was not the right fit, he and Martha wanted me to join Canadian Tire as president of the Foundation for Families. I was intrigued. They wanted me to build the foundation as something that would be embraced by both dealers and customers across the country. Such an opportunity does not come often. And the chance not only to raise money but also to give it away had real appeal. I signed on.

Research showed that most Canadians knew and loved Canadian Tire. It is where we all went to get our first bike, skates, or hockey stick. And there is a Canadian Tire store in practically every community. Canadians also believed that Canadian Tire was a generous contributor to the community through the Foundation for Families. The problem was that people did not know what the Foundation for Families really supported. People did know that the CIBC Run for the Cure supported breast cancer.

My predecessor had done research that indicated that Canadians had a positive image of Canadian Tire in the field of sport and recreation. This could well serve as a sweet spot for Canadian Tire, and that seemed like a good starting point.

We went to work. First we brought together some experts in the field for brainstorming sessions, including people such as Dr. Bruce Kidd, then dean of the Faculty of Physical Education and Health at the University of Toronto. We learned that obesity among young people was seriously on the rise. We learned that physical activity among young people was in serious decline, both inside and outside of school. We learned that one of the reasons for low participation in sport and physical activities was that parents could not afford the cost of registration and equipment. Everyone we talked to felt that Canadian Tire could champion this cause.

The next thing was to discover what else was going on out there that might meet this need. We learned quickly of an organization called KidSport that was helping kids participate in sports. We went to a meeting in Ottawa with officials from the federal government working in this area and met some key staff members from KidSport, including Peter Quevillon from British Columbia. Sport BC owned the name KidSport. There was clearly real synergy at this meeting, and it struck us that this might make a great partner for Canadian Tire.

Mike Medline, a senior executive of and future president of Canadian Tire, and I went out to meet with senior board members of KidSport to explore the idea of a joint initiative going forward. A stumbling block was our desire that Canadian Tire have their name up front for branding purposes. Despite strong efforts from both sides, we both concluded that we were not able to bring about a merger, but we all agreed that we could and would work together.

By this time, we at Canadian Tire believed that the idea of getting kids involved in sport and recreation was rock solid. So we decided to see how we could make it work.

The next step was to meet and talk with local parks and recreation departments and with youth-serving agencies, like the YMCA, Boys and Girls Clubs, and Big Brothers and Big Sisters. We also talked to Canadian Tire store managers across the country.

After all our consultations, we developed a model that worked like this: With support from the foundation, in every Canadian Tire community, the local dealer or dealers would assemble a local chapter comprised of the leaders of local youth-serving agencies, municipal recreation departments, and so on. The steering committee, chaired by the local Canadian Tire dealer, would invite applications from parents for funds to cover the cost of registration and equipment to allow their kids to participate in whatever activity they chose. The steering committee would then allocate the money.

We first piloted the programme in the Niagara and St. Catharines area with our local dealers and Mary Turner from Canadian Tire Financial Services. It worked really well.

Dealers were happy because the chapters were locally based. This gave them an opportunity to lead the foundation's initiative in their own communities. And the money was being spent in their local community. The agencies were happy, as money would be getting out to kids in need in their communities.

With the success of the pilots, we were ready to launch the programme nationally. The key in any national signature programme is to come up with a name that works. I was part of that earlier with Take Our Kids to Work.

Often when creating a name or a brand, you hire an outside agency to do focus groups and research a variety of options. Prior to that a few of us were brainstorming ideas and one of us said we really need to Jumpstart this programme. That stopped the discussion. We looked at each other and said, "That's the name!"

We did focus group the name and found it worked with both employees and customers. It was like a new beginning. We loved it, and for Canadian Tire it had the added benefit of connecting with its automobile roots … jumpstarting a car.

Our lawyer went to work, and soon we had the trademark for Canadian Tire Jump Start. Before a formal launch, we had to think through how we would raise money. Canadian Tire agreed to cover all administrative costs. The Government of Canada and a few provincial governments agreed to support the programme.

We launched with a skating event, The Great Skate, on the Rideau Canal in Ottawa. Former Olympians Barbara Underhill and Paul Martini performed, and people from across Canada were invited to skate. It was a grand day.

We were convinced that employees would get excited about the programme and support it. The dealers said we could count on them. The question was how to get the customers involved. Giving at the cash register always has great potential, but we were looking for an idea that would allow the customer to also embrace the idea of physical activity.

Someone on the staff suggested that we sell a tennis ball at the cash register. People liked the idea, but we did not feel that a tennis ball was unique. I suggested we have a red tennis ball. That is, after all, Canadian Tire's colour, and nobody has a red tennis ball.

Nothing is ever simple though. A couple of years earlier, Johann Koss, the famous Olympian, had founded the organization Right to Play, which encourages young people in developing countries to get active in play. He was using a red soccer ball as its logo.

I had met him once before and saw great value in Right to Play. That said, he was mightily upset with us selling red tennis balls. He asked to meet and arrived at my office the day we were selling red tennis balls at head office. This did not help the beginning of our meeting.

He made it very clear that since Right to Play "owned" the red soccer ball, we were infringing on their brand. He told me that his lawyer would be sending us a letter instructing or asking us, I was not sure which, to stop producing red tennis balls. It was not a pleasant meeting.

I chatted with President Wayne Sales. He said, "Gordon we have used the colour red at Canadian Tire for many years — I look forward to receiving the letter." Then I learned an important lesson on how the corporate world works. The lawyer volunteering with Right to

Play was Ralph Lean, a high-profile political fundraiser. He worked then for Cassels Brock, coincidentally the legal firm doing Canadian Tire's legal work. The letter, having been sent, was quickly withdrawn. End of story. Except for one thing. As of today, millions of dollars have been raised selling those little red Jump Start tennis balls. We have more than a few in our house.

Governments saw value in supporting Jump Start too. In the first year, funds were received from the Canadian government, the Ontario government, and the Government of Newfoundland and Labrador.

Today Canadian Tire Jump Start is an established, well-known brand clear across Canada. More important, through 289 chapters across the country, Jump Start has helped over 3 million kids participate in over seventy activities.

Canadian Tire Jump Start Charities is now alive in communities large and small right across Canada.

Jump Start succeeds because it works.

It works for dealers and employees who give their time and money to the programme and proudly wear their Jump Start T-shirt.

It works for customers who support and donate to Jump Start.

It works for youth-serving organizations across the country that deliver sport and recreation programming.

It works, most of all, for the young people who benefit from participating in sport and recreation. Before Jump Start, many young people could not afford to participate.

A feel-good story with enormous impact. A powerful combination that.

It was exciting to be involved at the beginning of Jump Start. But the real credit goes to those who continue to grow, build, and nurture Jump Start. Credit to Martha Billes, the founder of the foundation, who oversaw its evolution to Jump Start. In her role as chair emeritus, she continues to be a staunch supporter of giving equal opportunities for play to kids across Canada.

In 2025, Jump Start turns twenty. A cause worth celebrating.

Thoughts and Opinions

Awards and Recognition —You Are Not as Good as You Think You Are

Awards and recognition are affirming. For a moment, different organizations say nice things about you. You receive a plaque, and you hang it on the wall. It is all very nice, but then it is over.

Over the last fifty years, I have had my fair share, ranging from the Centennial Medal in 1967 to the Order of Ontario in 2016, and including an honorary doctorate in education.

The ones that have meant the most to me connect to my work with diverse communities, like the Urban Alliance on Race Relations Award, the African Canadian Achievement Award, or the Yee Hong Centre for Geriatric Care's Golden Achievement Award.

My first award in 1967, the Centennial Medal, had an unexpected twist.

I was in my first year at the School of Social Work. I came home to discover a small package in the mail. Turned out it was the Centennial Medal. I had no idea how I got it! Still do not. My roommates, Peter Turner and Wally Seccombe, thought it was great fun, and we celebrated by having fish and chips from the corner store.

Wally went up to his parents' house that evening. His father, Wally Seccombe Sr., had received the Centennial Medal that day, honouring his work in the community and for working with the YMCA to establish the YES Programme (Youth Employment Service). He was complaining that they only gave these recognition awards to old people, and Wally countered that I had received the same award that very day.

The next evening, I received a phone call from a reporter saying that he had just discovered I was the youngest winner of the Centennial Medal in Canada. I got excited. He told me that the *Toronto Star* wanted to do a feature article on me. I thought, *Wow, this is big-league stuff!*

He told me they were working on a theme for the article, and he wanted to test an idea out on me. I said, "Bring it on." He said they wanted to use the theme "a young man who peaked too soon." The wind went out of my sails in an instant. Then he said, "Gordon, it's Wally Seccombe's dad calling!" That did it. After a pause, we both had a good laugh.

One award does stand out for me. When I was leaving my job as vice president of U of T, the Alumni Association wanted to create an award in my honour. The idea was to focus on student community service and leadership rather than on academics. The Gordon Cressy Student Leadership Award would be given each year to several students from each faculty in their graduating year.

I was quite taken with the idea as it squared completely with my values. There was no money attached to the award; it was just a certificate. To be honest, we had no idea how it would work or even if people would show up to the award ceremony. The first couple of years, the ceremony was held at the university president's house. The turnout was fantastic. The students loved the award!

One of the students suggested that parents be invited to attend the following year. They came in large numbers. The award was so popular that the setting had to be changed, first to Hart House and then to Convocation Hall.

Each year I attended the ceremony, I got to speak briefly to this incredible group of student leaders and their family members. Watching these graduating students come across stage and learning of their enormous contributions to the university or the wider community was very moving. I left always feeling better about the future of the world. One of my proudest moments was in 1997, when my daughter Jillian won the award for her leadership in the Faculty of Physical and Health Education.

One year, I was heading off for the award ceremony and went downstairs to the washroom beforehand. As I was in my cubicle, I overheard two students talking. One said to the other, "Who the hell is this Gordon Cressy guy anyway?" The other responded, "I have absolutely no idea, but he must be really old or dead." I filed that remark away and headed back upstairs to the main hall.

As I entered, another student came up to me and said, "So you are Gordon Cressy!" He followed up with, "I just checked you out on Google and there are over three hundred references to you."

"Really," I said.

"Absolutely," he replied. "The problem is that over two hundred of them are people who have won the Gordon Cressy Award! Obviously, you were nothing until this award was created."

I filed this away too. When it came time for my remarks, I decided to talk about humility — a tough lesson that has sunk in.

Selfie with Ashley Bo Zhang.

Today, over 4,000 students have won this award.

After twenty-five years, it was time to refresh the event, and in 2020, the university replaced the Gordon Cressy Award with the U of T Student Leadership Award.

Listen to Your Kids

My dad taught my brothers and me to play golf. His dad taught him.

I was doing the same for my boys, Joseph and Keith. Joseph, being the better athlete and more competitive, took to golf immediately. Keith, less so. Keith is kind, creative, smart, and funnier than you can imagine, but golf … not so much! But he was always willing to try.

When he was five, I decided he was ready to play on a real golf course. So off we went to Blairhampton, the golf course near our cottage. We got through the first hole just fine and Keith was hitting the ball quite well. The second hole is a short par three over a small river. I hit a lovely shot about ten feet from the hole and was looking at a potential birdie. Keith hit it into the riverbank.

I know I should have gone with him to look for the ball, but I was excited about my birdie possibility and went directly to the green to size up my putt. Keith was down by the river, looking for the ball. I looked up and saw people waiting back on the tee for us to finish. I shouted, "Keith, hurry up!" Nothing happened. I shouted again, a little louder this time. Then Keith called out to me, "Dad, come quick!" I ran back to the river, thinking maybe Keith had found a couple of golf balls.

When I arrived, Keith proudly turned to me and said, "Dad, look at this really big frog!" It was in that moment that I realized it was discovering the frog that was important and not the golf game. Over the years, Keith did learn to play golf and plays with me from time to time. Though I think for him, the big frog is still more important.

Public Speaking

It all started with my dad.

He was always upbeat, enthusiastic, and full of positive energy.

When my brothers and I were very young, he told us to look adults in the eye when we spoke to them. I remember him practising speeches in front of the mirror. He used big words like "emulate" and "augur well."

In Grade 11, there was a high school public-speaking competition. I decided to enter.

We used to play ball hockey on our corner street, Bocastle. One of the guys who played was Brian Conacher from the famous Conacher sports family.

Brian played for the Toronto Maple Leafs and on Canada's gold medal Olympic team. His father, Lionel, was voted Canada's athlete of the half century 1900–1950. He played at the highest levels in hockey, baseball, lacrosse, and football and, in addition, was a successful politician.

I did some research on Lionel Conacher (it was on microfiche in those days) and made my speech the Lionel Conacher story. It went over very well with the audience, although I did not win. But I was hooked. I remember that speech to this day, and if asked can tell it like it was the first time.

Over the years, I spoke more and more. I never took a course, but I learned that being authentic and telling real stories connected. I have never used a PowerPoint presentation. It seems to me connecting with the audience is important from the get-go. For me, a good start with humour gets me going and relaxes the audience and, to be frank, relaxes me too.

This is an example of an opening I have used for years. It really works, but in truth I made it up completely.

I was in Chicago giving a speech to a business audience on the growing topic of corporate social responsibility. Just before the speech I was walking down the corridor beside another gentleman. He turned to me and said, "Are you going back in for the keynote speech?"

Obviously, he did not know who I was — and why should he?

I responded with, "Absolutely — what about you?"

He said, "I don't think so."

I asked, "Why not?"

He said, "Well, who wants to listen to some social worker from Canada talk about corporate social responsibility?"

I looked directly at him and said, "You think you got problems?"

He came back with, "What do you mean?"

I said, "Look, all you have to do is listen — I have to speak."

He decided to come to the talk after all.

A great beginning sets the stage for the whole talk, as it brings people in.

A bad beginning can set things off for the whole talk.

When I was at the United Way, I would often speak three or four times a day to employee groups. To be honest, the tough part was not the talk but getting from place to place on time.

One morning, I rushed to the second event. Audrey Wakelin, a volunteer well into her eighties, had set the stage very well for me.

(She was retired from the Ontario government and, for many years, was a champion volunteer speaker for the United Way.)

I opened, as I did many fundraising speeches, with the well-known story of a hen and a pig who lived on a farm. One day they went outside to explore the countryside and came to a little church with a sign saying, "Give to Help the Poor." The hen and pig thought about what they could do to help. The hen said, "Let's donate bacon and eggs!"

The pig thought about it and blurted out, "Well, that is fine for you, that is a just a contribution, but for me it's a total commitment!"

I would follow with, "And this morning I am here to talk about contributions."

This joke, even though a few people had heard it before, always worked.

Not this morning though — no one laughed. I was completely thrown for the duration of my remarks. I just could not get back on track.

I was crushed. As I was leaving, I leaned over and asked one of the people in the audience what I had done wrong. He looked up at me and said, "You stole the old lady's joke. She told it and it was funny. But you came up and repeated it — that is not funny."

Another lesson learned. Know what goes on before you arrive.

In my speeches, I would develop messages or stories that fit to the audience. I would often arrive early and chat with some members of the audience and ask what they would like to hear.

I learned that self-deprecating humour works very well.

I learned that telling personal stories connects.

I learned I could be funny and sad, and people could both laugh and shed tears.

I have had the opportunity to speak in every province in Canada, a few cities in the U.S., and a couple of times in the Far East, in some African countries, and many times in Trinidad and Tobago. It has been a fantastic run for me.

I reached a point where I no longer needed notes or cards, just took the microphone and went to work.

I had this view, echoed in a wonderful book by Canadian Keith Spicer called *Winging It*, that if you had a strong opening and a strong close and told stories and the lessons from the stories, the speech would work. I would do my preparation before the speech and then leave the paper when I went to the podium.

There was a calm and quiet confidence at work beneath the surface. I operated with the knowledge that, if I missed, the only person who would know would be me. At the end, I am most often energized by the talk.

I have had the opportunity to speak to groups of anywhere from 10 to 1,500 people. Whatever the number, the goal is to give the audience a great experience. Leave them wanting more. Do not go on too long. My father always said, no one ever complained about a speech being too short.

When I first started out, over forty years ago, I would often receive a pen or a gift certificate or a book. Then, for a couple of decades, I was paid real money. Now I am back to pens and gift certificates. That is as it should be.

Closing Time

The key to a really good speech is how it ends. You want people to leave feeling great and wanting more.

I usually close my speeches by returning to the theme of my remarks and a powerful quote. To teachers, the group I spoke to most often, I would paraphrase a quote by Chinese philosopher Lao Tzu:

> Go to the young people,
> Live with them and love them
> Start with what they know.
> Build on what they have.
> But when the job is done,
> The task accomplished,
> The young people all say
> We did it ourselves.

I then say, moving young people from dependence to independence is noble work. That is what you teachers do every day. I end with a simple thank you.

In the last few years, I have spoken to more seniors' groups. Probably because I am a senior myself.

I usually take people down memory lane with splashes of humour. Then I share with them this poem, "Around the Corner," my dad gave me when he retired.

Around the corner I have a friend,
In this great city that has no end;
Yet days go by, and weeks rush on,
And before I know it, a year is gone,
And I never see my old friend's face,
For Life is a swift and terrible race.
He knows I like him just as well
As in the days when I rang his bell
And he rang mine. We were younger then,
And now we are busy, tired men:
Tired with playing a foolish game,
Tired with trying to make a name.
"Tomorrow," I say, "I will call on Jim,
Just to show that I'm thinking of him."
But tomorrow comes—and tomorrow goes,
And the distances between us grows and grows.
Around the corner! yet miles away...
"Here's a telegram, sir..."
        "Jim died today."
And that's what we get, and deserve in the end:
Around the corner, a vanished friend.

—"Around the Corner," Charles Hanson Towne

After this, I issue the challenge to not forget about the Jims in each of our lives.

At the end, people often come to share with me their stories and tell me they are going right home to connect with the Jim they miss…

The chance to be out on stage with a microphone still excites.

I hope to keep doing this for many years to come.

Golf and Private Golf Courses: The Last Bastion of Privilege

I grew up loving golf. Together with my two brothers and my dad we played a lot, sometimes together but often with other friends. We competed at our home course, Rosedale, and my brother Bill won the club championship twice. He was successful at provincial and Canadian tournaments. My dad, too, in his early days won his share of local club events. In 1966, at the Royal Montreal Golf Course, we won the quite amazing Canadian Father and Three Sons Golf Tournament! That was a proud moment. Sadly, after Bill's all too early death, we were no longer able to play in that event.

One year, I think it was 1967, Bill was in the final of the Rosedale Golf Club Championship against Gordon Stollery, who founded Angus Glen Golf Club many years later. In those days, members and their friends would walk around and watch the match. I had invited my friend Jim Bascombe from Trinidad, who had worked with me at the YMCA and was visiting the Toronto Y to do some basketball coaching.

Bill played well, but Gord Stollery was better that day and won the championship. As always happens, the winner invited all of us into the clubhouse for an after-match drink. There were maybe thirty of us in total.

After a few minutes, the general manager signalled me to come over. He said, "Who is that Black person over there?" I was momentarily stunned but said in a confident voice that it was my friend James Bascombe from Trinidad, who was up visiting the YMCA. The manager said, "The members do not want him in here and he must leave." I went over to talk with my dad, who at that time served on the board of directors of Rosedale. I was angry about this and embarrassed for my friend James. My dad did not like conflict in public. Although he disagreed with the manager, he suggested that James and I should leave. We did.

The next day, James was being honoured at the downtown YMCA. I was with him and the head of the YMCA, Bill Naylor, when two members from Rosedale, who I had seen there the day before, emerged from the health club.

Bill Naylor stopped these two members and in glowing terms introduced James Bascombe. Much to my surprise, they were very polite.

That night I asked my dad about the huge contrast in experiences. He used the words "turf protection." He explained that when people are in their own territory, they often behave differently than when they are in someone else's territory. I did not like it and shortly thereafter I resigned from Rosedale. It was the right thing to do.

I still see my friend James Bascombe when I visit Trinidad. For many years, he served as the driver for the Canadian high commissioner in Trinidad. Fortunately, we can reflect and laugh about the time he was asked to leave the golf club.

Despite this, my father loved golf, and he loved Rosedale. In 1997, he was made an honorary life member for fifty years' membership and service to the club.

Some would say, "Oh well, that was a long time ago," and it was. But change at Rosedale came slowly.

George Cohon, the then distinguished president of McDonald's Restaurants of Canada and the man credited with saving the Santa Claus Parade, had applied to join Rosedale in the early 2000s. He had the perfect Rosedale pedigree, save for the fact he was Jewish. And he was rightly proud of it. The old blackball system was at play, and George Cohon's application was rejected. The *Globe and Mail* got wind of this and covered the story. Fortunately, some of the long-standing members, including the father of John Tory (former mayor of Toronto), saw the potential problem, and George Cohon quietly withdrew his application until a new and more inclusive membership approval process was in place. George eventually became the first Jewish member of Rosedale.

The Toronto Hunt Golf Club

For almost twenty years after leaving Rosedale, I played mostly pickup golf at pay-as-you-play courses. I was busy with other priorities — work and family.

In the mid-1980s my wife's uncle, Frank McGee, a former Conservative politician who was a descendant of Father of Confederation Thomas D'Arcy McGee, suggested I join the Toronto Hunt, where he was a member.

An interesting tidbit here is that Sir John A. Macdonald passed on the crib that he had used to raise his kids to Thomas D'Arcy McGee, and that crib was passed on to family members through the years. Both our sons, Joseph and Keith, were raised in that very crib. I told this story to former Ontario Premier Bill Davis. When introducing me at an event, he said he hoped my boys would come back to the Conservative fold being raised in John A. Macdonald's crib! Sorry to report to all the Conservatives out there — no such luck!

In 1986, I did join the Toronto Hunt. I loved the nine-hole course overlooking the Scarborough Bluffs. And I was proud that year to win the club championship. We had many happy times on and off the golf course. We celebrated my parents' fiftieth wedding anniversary there, and my boys loved the sundaes at the Sunday brunch. We donated a trophy in my father's honour to help create the parent-and-child tournament, and then my son Joseph and I won the tournament three times.

That said, I was always a bit nervous that my experience at Rosedale might happen at the Toronto Hunt. I remember one time there was a major United Way conference in Toronto, with delegates from all over the United States. I agreed to take three Black friends to play golf at the Toronto Hunt as my guests. When I went to pick them up at the hotel, they were all wearing short-shorts. I realized I had a serious problem. Golf clubs are notorious for tough dress codes. One rule is no short-shorts. Shorts must be Bermuda length. I was ready, if need be, to fight the racism but not the dress code! They changed into long pants, and we went and had a very good time with no incidents.

A couple of years later, it did not go so well. I was at the University of Toronto, and we were honouring two large donors from Hong Kong, Mr. Cheng Yu-tung and Mr. Lee Shau-kee. They were both billionaire businessmen and they loved golf. I suggested to Rob Prichard, then president of U of T, that we take them to the Toronto Hunt and play golf. We four were having a great time on the course. Our guests had very limited English, but we got along just fine. And the universal sign of thumbs-up for a good shot worked well.

On the seventeenth hole, we were waiting to tee off when two golfers came up beside us. One of them said in a very loud voice, "If your guests can't speak English they should not be allowed on the course." By that time, Cheng Yu-tung's son-in-law, William Doo, a U of T grad, had joined us. He turned to me and in an elegant way just said, "You must be embarrassed by the behaviour of your fellow members." I do not know if William Doo ever told his father-in-law and Lee Shau-kee what happened. This time, though, I took some action. I wrote a formal complaint to the club general manager and used William Doo's thoughtful words to describe the incident. The club took the complaint seriously, and the two members in question got a letter reprimanding them for their comments.

My wife's uncle, Frank McGee, also got in on the act. He thought it time that the club revise its by-laws to explicitly and formally state that membership was open to anyone — it would not discriminate on the grounds of race, creed, or sexual orientation. This passed unanimously. He also thought it would be neat if the lieutenant governor was made an honorary member. The fact that the lieutenant governor at that time, the enormously popular Lincoln Alexander, was Black was an important signal to the community that things were changing.

The Toronto Hunt gained a great deal of its revenue from member-sponsored parties. It was a fantastic setting overlooking Lake Ontario, with free parking, and was a popular wedding venue. A friend, originally from Trinidad, Hyacinth Tackoor, asked if her daughter Jacintha could get married at the club. I happily sponsored the event. Jacintha was Christian of East Indian background. Her husband-to-be was originally from Jordan and was of the Muslim faith.

The late-spring wedding was to be outside, with the reception to follow inside. Unfortunately, on the day of the wedding, it was cold and rainy. The staff recommended that the wedding be moved inside and asked the few members of the club who were in the large dining room to move to the small adjacent room to have lunch. The members were none too happy about this. Maybe it was just the fact of being moved. I suspect for some it had to do with the guests attending the wedding.

My wife and I and two other couples were the only white people in the room. The others were of East Indian and African heritage, as well as Jordanian. The husband's family, who had arrived from Jordan, were all wearing traditional Jordanian clothing.

I could feel tension rising. One of the guests was Lieutenant Governor Lincoln Alexander. I went right over to him and suggested that he accompany me to the washroom. I had a plan. He said he did not need to go, but off we went anyway. As we passed the small dining area, the members saw Lincoln Alexander and stood up out of respect. One of the members said, "Your Honour, it is so nice to see you — why are you here?" He responded he was attending this fascinating wedding between this young woman of Trinidadian heritage and a young Muslim man originally from Jordan, and the ceremony was to be a blend of both religious traditions.

Immediately, a couple of the members asked if they could watch. Soon after, many more came to watch. I realized I could never have made that happen — but Lincoln Alexander did. If you cannot do it yourself, find someone who can. A powerful lesson learned. It was a great wedding. And private golf courses are slow to change — but they are changing.

Frugality — Or You Really Are a Cheapskate

I have always been cheap — or *frugal*, which is a better-sounding word.

Part of that is personal. I always look for the free or cheapest place to park. When we went on a family trip to Disneyland, I was endlessly dragging Joanne and our boys off to look at timeshare promotions so we could get the free coupons to Disney attractions. I once took a case of Diet Coke to the Dominican Republic on a family holiday to avoid paying hotel prices for my favourite drink. I told my wife that I had a coupon for laser eye surgery — "two eyes for the price of one!" This did not go over very well ... she said I was putting my eyes at risk, and when I insisted on proceeding, in protest, she refused to pick me up after the surgery!

In my work life, I believed very strongly that staff should be very careful in charging expenses, particularly when using donor dollars.

Sometimes it worked; sometimes not so much.

Once, when I was chair of the Toronto Board of Education, I arranged to meet with Joe Grittani, my counterpart at the Toronto Separate School Board, to discuss the thorny topic of sharing schools.

Duncan Green, director of education at the Toronto Board, asked where I was planning to meet him. I told him experience had taught me that breaking bread together was better than a straight-up meeting, as we would get to know each other. Duncan agreed and politely inquired where I planned to take him. I told him Swiss Chalet, my favourite restaurant. He quickly set me straight, letting me know that Joe Grittani was a wealthy man of Italian heritage. Duncan suggested that I take him to a nice Italian restaurant like La Scala on Bay Street. Swiss Chalet would just not cut it. We went to La Scala and had a nice time. But we did not make too much progress on sharing schools.

Soon after I was appointed president of the United Way of Greater Toronto, Paul Winnell, our area-wide director, and I had a meeting with the heads of the six surrounding United Ways. After the meeting we adjourned to the Fisherman's Wharf for lunch.

After lunch, the waiter brought the bill for $80 (things were cheaper in 1982). I looked at it and asked that each person contribute $10, and I would pay the tip. I thought that was a nice gesture on my part. There was a long pause, and then each person slowly passed me $10. I sensed some reluctance to give me the money, and I was confused.

After the meeting, I asked Paul if I had done something wrong. He noted that my predecessor had always paid for everybody, charging it to the United Way. I asked him why we would pay for staff to have lunch with each other. He simply said, "That's the way it has always been done." I said, "Well that's the end of that," and asked Paul if I should get in contact with each of them to explain this new policy.

Paul gave me a sly smile and simply said, "I think you already have!" We never had that problem again.

Sharing Gifts and Recognizing and Thanking People

At U of T, I was quite a stickler about not spending too much money on gifts or tokens to visitors and donors. I was new to culturally appropriate gift exchanges.

This became a contentious and serious issue when one of our vice presidents returned from a trip to Japan, clearly upset. I asked her what had gone wrong. She said the distinguished president of a major university in Japan had given her a jade bracelet, and she had given him a U of T coffee mug! She was embarrassed and not happy ... and she was correct.

We explored a few different options. Many people in Asia love golf. And Titleist is by far the most popular golf ball. We decided on a great gift, a package of Titleist golf balls stamped with the U of T logo. People loved it — and it was not terribly expensive. We still hear of people finding U of T golf balls in Hong Kong, China, Malaysia, Singapore, Japan, and Taiwan. Amazing!

The Tobago Years, 2008–2010

Getting There

Over the years, I made many trips to Trinidad and Tobago and made a point of bringing each member of my family — my first wife, Marsha; my wife, Joanne; my children, Jennifer, Jillian, Joseph, and Keith; and my brother Jim — on a "pilgrimage" to visit this place that had meant so much to me. Sometimes the trips were volunteer related; sometimes we just went for a holiday.

Joanne, who had volunteered with CUSO in Zambia from 1974 to 1977, had always talked about doing community service work abroad after we retired. In the spring of 2007, we were visiting Trinidad and chatted with our good friend, Howard Sabga, who was the chair of the Trinidad YMCA. He said they had never had a formal YMCA in Tobago and suggested that we come to Tobago for three years and work with the community to build a Y.

We took a deep breath, talked with our family, retired from our jobs, and then said, "Let's do it!" Howard added one wrinkle — the Trinidad Y had no money to pay for this.

Well, we like challenges. We talked to some friends about supporting this initiative and got lots of encouragement. Our dear friend Allan Slaight said he wanted to make the first gift and he sent $10,000. The Toronto YMCA agreed to give tax receipts and to host a combined fundraiser and send-off event in late fall 2007.

We called it "Joanne and Gordon's Excellent Adventure," and we invited everyone we knew to come to our event at the Y and to donate to the cause. We had a steel band from Jesse Ketchum School, well-known Calypso singer Macomere Fifi, originally from Tobago, and various speakers, including David Crombie, Bob Rae, Paul Garfinkel, Joseph Wong, Harold Brathwaite, and Shirley Hoy, who said nice things about us. Howard Sabga and his wife, Jackie, flew up to Toronto for the event. Much to our surprise we raised $128,000 as seed money for our project.

Getting Going...

We rented a house, bought a used car, and set out to meet people. We really had no contacts in Tobago.

The first person we met with was Norris Jack, the principal advisor to Orville London (chief secretary of the Tobago House of Assembly). We immediately liked each other. Norris Jack became a dear friend and mentor to us throughout the project. Sadly, he passed away a few years ago from cancer. Norris liked the idea of a Y in Tobago and encouraged us to make a courtesy call on Chief Secretary and Assemblyman Claudia Groome-Duke, the head of Education, Youth Affairs, and Sport.

So off we went to meet with Orville London, the smart, distinguished head of the Tobago government. Thinking back, I am sure he has seen the likes of us come and go many times in Tobago — retirees wanting to "make a difference" without much sense of Tobago or its people. He listened patiently to our enthusiastic pitch and wished us well. It was a brushoff, but a very pleasant one.

When we met with Norris Jack, we told him that we intended to form a local steering committee to oversee the project. Norris, without hesitation, said that we must get Dr. Eastlyn McKenzie involved. At the same time, our dear friend Zally Hassanali, the former first lady of Trinidad and Tobago, also advised us to get in touch with Dr. McKenzie, saying that Eastlyn knew everybody and everybody liked her.

We soon discovered the magic of Dr. Eastlyn McKenzie. She came over, bounded into our house, and we talked and talked. Eastlyn has a doctorate in Adult Education and spent her entire career working in Tobago, doing mostly community-development work. She also served as an independent in the Trinidad and Tobago Senate. She was well over sixty-five, and exuded warmth and energy. We could tell she could get things done. She knew everybody and was quick to tell us who were the talkers and who were the doers. She was clearly sizing us up too.

Near the end of our meeting, she said, "Count me in!" She agreed to chair our steering committee and to be the public face for the new YMCA.

Getting Involved in the Community

We knew that we would have to earn it in the community. After all, Tobagonians had seen more than their share of white "do-gooders" come and go over the years.

We chose to focus on the local Tobago community. Soon after we arrived, we discovered the Tobago Aqua Joggers, a group of mostly seniors who, three mornings a week, do aqua fitness in the Caribbean Sea, starting at — wait for it — 5:30 a.m.! We loved it and went every Monday, Wednesday, and Friday morning. After finishing our exercises, which we all numbered off together, we swam in a circle chanting, "Every single cell in my body is healthy!" Most of the people could not swim but wore aqua-fitness belts to keep them afloat. Joanne signed on as secretary. Our monthly meetings were held before going into the sea in the early morning. And, of course, our meetings always started with a prayer. As a matter of fact, every meeting in Tobago started with a prayer.

When we realized that virtually no one could actually swim, I thought it might be fun to start a learn-to-swim class at the pool where we lived. It is difficult to learn to swim in the sea because of the waves and currents.

People did not know the name Cressy, so instead I decided to call it "Mr. Gordon's Adult Swim School." We made up a short flyer, which we handed out at the next Aqua Joggers meeting. At first, I wanted to do it for free, but that idea did not go over very well. People wanted to pay something. So we had a ten-lesson package for about Can$1.50 a lesson, with the condition that, if you could not swim the length of the pool in ten lessons, you got your money back! Encouraged by the participants, Joanne kept a careful accounting of who had and had not paid, and I set about to teach them to swim. In the end, everyone did manage to swim the length, and we had a certificate presentation and a celebratory dinner at our place.

We were making friends.

Carnival

Shortly after we arrived, it was Carnival time in Trinidad and Tobago, and we decided that we would participate. We figured that, if we were going to do it, we had to go all the way, or as Joanne liked to say, "In for a penny, in for a pound." We went to the steel band competition and to the Calypso tent. We loved the performers, and the atmosphere was upbeat and friendly. Of course, Trinidad has a huge Carnival celebration with large numbers of tourists, but in Tobago, Carnival is local.

Early on Carnival Monday morning, we got up at four o'clock and went to participate in J'ouvert. During J'ouvert the streets are full of people dancing and "wining" (a rather sexy grinding dance where you press up against whoever happens to be dancing next to you) through the streets to the blaring "road march" music. Everyone wears old T-shirts and shorts because people throw huge amounts of paint everywhere. We had a blast. We laughed, wined, and drank too much. When it was over, we threw ourselves into the sea to wash off.

Tuesday is when you play mas with your chosen band. We signed up with a band named Ashante Ananse in the town of Buccoo. Joanne volunteered to help make the costumes and spent many days helping construct gorgeous papier-mâché characters. And we made friends. Many bands in Carnival have people parading the streets in skimpy bikinis and beads. That was not for us, so we chose a band with more traditional costumes.

On Carnival morning, we arrived in our costumes at the Tamarind Square car park on the outskirts of the capital city of Scarborough. I had been advised not to carry anything while participating in Carnival, so I left my wallet, cellphone, and house keys locked in our car.

What to do with my car key? I decided that, since my costume had no pockets, I would just put the key in my underwear! Big mistake…

We were having a great time dancing with our band through the streets of Scarborough; music was blaring. About halfway through, I realized that the car key was gone. I decided that since Joanne was having such a good time, best not to tell her till the end. About 9:00 p.m., our band wound its way back up the hill to the car park, and after hugs all around, we went our separate ways. By the way, we won the medium band competition!

It was at this point that I turned to Joanne and said, "We have a problem!" She was still basking in the joy of Carnival and said, "And what is the problem that WE have?" I told her about the keys and how I put them in my underwear and now they were gone. She looked incredulous and just said, "You put the keys where?"

This clearly was not a relationship-enhancing move. However, we got it together and decided that the best thing to do was to visit the nearby police station.

Remember, this was Carnival Tuesday, and all sorts of things were going on. In we marched in full costume, sensing that a lost key was hardly on their priority list. But we talked with a kind officer who wanted to be helpful. He listened patiently and then said he would get one of his junior officers to drive us home. I thanked him but said, unfortunately, our house keys were still in the car.

He then said he knew a locksmith who owned a store aptly named the Pry Master, and he gave him a call. The Pry Master agreed to come out, and we met him fifteen minutes later at the car. He did the old coat hanger down the inside window of the car and, presto, it was opened.

We got our wallet, purse, house keys, cellphone, and camera. He took out the lock for the car and said early in the morning he would go into work and make a new key for the car.

He then kindly dropped us home. He asked us to take a taxi to his store in the morning. Early the next morning, he phoned to say that he had a new key already made. He came up to our place and drove us to our car. His bill was very reasonable. This man wrote the book on customer service. If you are in Tobago and find yourself in need of a locksmith — call the Pry Master!

Getting the Land and Raising Money

During the initial six months, we used our basic training in community work. We thought of it as Community Development 101. We went out and met people. We met with everyone we could. Each person suggested several others we should get to know, and on it went. And we listened a lot.

What was clear was that most Tobagonians had never heard of the YMCA. But we quickly learned that the "C" in YMCA had particular resonance with people on the island, a very Christian place. The idea of a Christian organization that worked particularly with youth was appealing.

We met with a variety of organizations on the island, including the Rotary Club, the Chamber of Commerce, and community centres. We also met with faith community leaders and political leaders. We did a needs assessment. We recruited a founding steering committee that reflected the breadth and depth of the island, and of course the indefatigable Dr. Eastlyn McKenzie was the chair.

We quickly learned that there was not one public swimming pool on the island. Wealthy people had villas with pools, as did the high-end hotels. Although Tobago is surrounded by the sea with many beautiful beaches, it was estimated that over 70 percent of the island residents could not swim. The Tobago House of Assembly (THA) had already recognized the need for public pools and had plans on the books for a couple of swimming pools to be built. We suggested to the THA leadership that, rather than building the first pool themselves, they partner with the YMCA, with its internationally known Learn to Swim programmes, and together create the bold vision of "Every Child a Swimmer."

Lo and behold, they agreed! The Tobago House of Assembly said that they would put up the land on a long-term lease. Our steering committee members toured potential sites and locked in on a terrific one, three beautiful acres overlooking Courland Bay on the Caribbean Sea near the towns of Black Rock and Plymouth. We negotiated a thirty-year lease at nominal rent.

Around this time, Joanne and I attended a drug-and-alcohol conference in Tobago where we met one of the organizers, Anne Blache-Fraser. When I lived in Trinidad in the early 1960s, the treasurer of the YMCA was a wonderful man, Louis Blache-Fraser. I wondered if she was related to him. She told me that Louis was her father-in-law, and she invited us to visit. Louis Blache-Fraser had had a profound impact on me when I was young, and I had saved a letter he had written to me in 1964. When we visited, I showed this letter to his son Robert. He was touched by this.

Robert told me he was an architect; he immediately became interested in our project to build the YMCA aquatic centre in Tobago and offered to help. He saw it as a way to honour his father and offered to do the project for a substantial discount. We were on the move.

We went back to the government and showed them our preliminary plans. They were excited and assigned a senior person to liaise with us for the course of the project.

Now we had to figure out how to pay for the project. The preliminary costing came in at TT$12 million (about Can$2 million). Dr. McKenzie, my wife, and I then met again with the chief secretary and made what we thought was a compelling case: If the government would put up TT$6 million dollars, we would raise the rest. The chief secretary knew that Dr. McKenzie did not like to hear the word *no* … and he said yes.

Now we had a site, a large financial contribution from the government, and a beautiful design. But we had to raise a lot of money in a part of the world where fundraising large sums of money was extremely uncommon.

We decided to launch our fundraising campaign at the new and only movie theatre in Tobago, called Movietowne, which agreed to give us the theatre for free. We decided to show the Academy Award–nominated documentary film *Mandela: Son of Africa, Father of a Nation.*

I got in touch with our friend Pat van der Merwe from the Nelson Mandela Children's Fund in South Africa, and she arranged to have Nelson Mandela send a letter to Dr. McKenzie, congratulating the YMCA on this important initiative.

We sold out the movie and raised some significant money for the YMCA.

Nelson Mandela
CHILDREN'S FUND

CHANGING THE WAY SOCIETY TREATS ITS CHILDREN AND YOUTH

15 January 2009

Dr. Eastlyn McKenzie
Chairperson
YMCA Steering Committee Tobago
PO Box 1115
Bon Accord
Tobago West Indies.

Dear Dr. McKenzie,

Congratulations on starting up a new Young Men's Christian Association in beautiful Tobago! This brings back memories of my visit to Trinidad five years ago with Bishop Tutu to support South Africa's bid for the FIFA World Cup which, I am sure you all know by now, will take place in South Africa next year. Were I younger, I would have loved to join you in Tobago for the launch.

I understand you are formally launching the YMCA with the showing of the film "Mandela-Father of a Nation" – I do hope you enjoy the show.

The work of the YMCA focuses on developing strong young people, strong families, and strong communities. This approach augers well with the work of the Nelson Mandela Children's Fund which I started in South Africa in 1995 to change with way society treats our children and youth.

I hope that, as you begin your work today, your Association will provide the young people of Tobago with the skills and confidence today to become the country's leaders of tomorrow.

Sincerely

Mandela

NELSON MANDELA

Claude Benoît, a member of the YMCA steering committee and the owner of Tobago Channel Five, the local television station, agreed the following night to put the movie on TV so all Tobagonians could watch it. And at the bottom of the screen was a scroll asking people to phone in and pledge money to the YMCA. The next day, the movie theatre did not open until the evening, so we bussed high school kids to the theatre, where they paid a small fee. We had three different showings of the film, giving the students an opportunity to learn about this giant of a man — and to hear about our plans for a Y in Tobago.

All in, an impressive beginning.

Listen to the People

We cleared the pool site and began to excavate with large backhoes. As the work was proceeding, one of the workers came up to us and said, "This is terrific soil." I had no idea what he was talking about. He told me that everyone in Tobago has a garden, growing vegetables, fruits, and flowers, and he said, "We can sell this." I thought he was kidding ... but no. He said, "We could get feedbags donated and on one day have a great sale of dirt. People will buy this topsoil."

The feedbags were to come for free from San Fernando in the south of Trinidad. My old friend from the Trinidad Y, Bing Mandbodh, lived in the south and got them over to Tobago.

The trucking company that was working on our contract offered to donate their trucks for those who wanted large quantities of topsoil.

We got free advertising on the radio from George Leacock of Radio Tambrin, and Claude Benoît from Channel Five TV. We called the event "Topsoil Day for the YMCA."

Topsoil Day was to start at 9:00 a.m. on a Saturday, with many volunteers to do the shovelling. I still had no idea whether this would work or not. It certainly did not fit into my fundraising experience. At seven thirty in the morning, we got a call from the security guard telling us to "Get down here quick ... there are forty cars here and line-ups already!"

All day long, cars came, trucks too. We all shovelled and shovelled, and the people kept coming. We had music blaring, and throughout day, Radio Tambrin reported on the event, encouraging people to come down and get their soil. The media loved it. There was so much demand that we did it again the following weekend. We raised over TT$40,000 (about Can$8,000) selling topsoil and, just as important, everyone was getting excited about the YMCA and Tobago's first community pools. And more individual donations came in.

Picture: Eastlyn McKenzie and Joanne Campbell.

This is a nice story, but also important was the message it sent to corporate donors: The local community supports this. If people who have little give a little, then people who have a lot can give more.

This started to happen. The banks got onside. Our biggest breakthrough came via Hasely Crawford, Trinidad's Olympic Gold Medal winner in the 100 metres at the 1976 Games in Montreal. Hasely worked for the National Gas Company of Trinidad and Tobago, and worked to deliver our lead gift of TT$4 million.

The United Way came on board, as did the Canadian government through the Canadian International Development Agency. Many of our suppliers wanted to help as well and gave us donations in kind. A final gift from the Ministry of Sport and Youth Affairs in Trinidad allowed us to achieve our fundraising goal.

The project was completed on time and on budget.

We wanted to have the official opening of the pools at the end of August 2010, with a soft opening in July so that kids could attend a swimming summer camp.

We had a lot of work to do to complete the construction and to hire and train staff. We needed swim instructors, but there were not enough qualified people on the island. So we approached the Canadian YMCA, and Denise Yoreff, from the Y in St. Catharines, Ontario, came down free of charge for a week to conduct a swim instructor training and certification programme. We advertised in the local Tobago news, put up notices, and got a huge turnout of applicants for the training. Since our pool was still under construction, the Mount Irvine Hotel very kindly loaned us its pool, free of charge, to conduct the week-long training programme. Denise subsequently came back to Tobago two more times to recertify and to train new instructors.

We knew it would be touch and go to finish the construction of the pool, administration building, and changerooms on time. The workers were working hard but the deadline was looming. I did not know much about project management per se, but we knew being there every day and being encouraging and grateful were the right things to do.

We did get the pool open for Summer Swim Camp (which, by the way, was a HUGE success, with the highest enrollment of any of the summer camps). Following that, we closed the pool again to finish the construction and clean up any deficiencies.

Saturday, August 11, 2010, was the final of the World Cup of Football (we call it soccer) between Spain and the Netherlands, being played in Johannesburg, South Africa. Tobagonians love their football. One of their own, Dwight Yorke, is a national icon, having played for a couple of top European clubs. He also served as captain of the Trinidad and Tobago team that went to the World Cup for the first time in 2006. So, when Trinidad and Tobago tied Sweden in the opening match, the whole country was watching.

And the country was so excited for the World Cup final that the prime minister declared a national holiday. All Tobagonians and my wife and I were going to watch this final.

I went down to the pool just to see how things were going. On Saturdays and Sundays, we usually had a skeleton staff on duty.

Imagine my surprise when there were about ten men working!

I asked incredulously what they were doing at the pool rather than watching football. One of them looked up and said proudly, "It's our pool too, you know." That for me said it all. It was to be the community's pool.

Sunday, August 29, 2010, was the official opening of the YMCA.

The Bucco Buccaneers, one of the finest steel bands in Tobago, was going to perform. During the summer camp, Anne Marie Brimacombe had trained all the kids attending to sing K'naan's famous song "Waving Flag," as well as, of course, the Village People's "YMCA." There were going to be demonstrations in the pool and various speeches by dignitaries.

Our friend John Honderich, chair of the *Toronto Star*, came down to Tobago to visit and join us for the opening. The media had promised to cover the event. The weather forecast was great, with no rain called for. We were expecting a large turnout.

Everything was looking very good.

On the Saturday morning, the day before our big event, Joanne, John Honderich, and I were having breakfast on our porch, looking out over the Caribbean Sea. Suddenly, a man with a T-shirt covering most of his face leapt up onto our porch brandishing a cutlass, screaming at us.

I immediately got up and tried to make the point that we were the good guys, helping build a pool for the community. With that, he raised his arm and WHACKED me with flat side of the cutlass across the side of my face. This got my attention real fast, and it hurt too.

He then said, "Hush your mouth." We immediately knew that the most important thing was to be safe. It was clear that he wanted money. Joanne thought it best to calm the situation down and gave him a glass of water. We all gave him what cash we had on hand.

Then, because he had no transport, he demanded I drive him where he wanted to go. I did drive him to a nearby village, dropped him where he wanted, and got back home quickly. The police came and we were interviewed. The water glass was dusted for fingerprints. The fence where the suspect had broken in was fixed.

We were left more than a little traumatized by it all. We managed to go out to dinner at a friend's house. On Sunday morning, first thing, Chief Secretary Orville London dropped by to show his concern and offer his support.

Sunday's official opening was important, so we put the incident behind us and rose to the occasion. The event went off perfectly, and Tobagonians had every reason to be proud.

John Honderich planned to write an article for the *Toronto Star* about our wonderful time in Tobago. As a journalist, he saw this incident as something to include in the article. We felt this would cloud the overarching story and he agreed not to include it.

After a few days, Joanne and I simply carried on. The police investigation just seemed to run out of steam.

Then, in late October, after a dinner party, I was cleaning up outside when I was charged by a man with what looked like the same T-shirt. This time he was carrying a meat cleaver and smacked me hard on the ribs. I remember saying to myself, Here we go again. This time he took money and our laptop and made us drive to the bank and get money from the bank machine. We then dropped him off and he was gone.

We realized then we simply could not continue like this. We had the very uneasy feeling that we were now an easy target. Either we needed to upgrade security and get dogs or we had to call it a day. We had no interest in living in fear of being attacked, and we were not at all inclined to live with dogs barking at people and endless security measures. So, almost three years to the day from our arrival, we knew it was time to head home. Our family missed us, and we missed our family.

We had come for three years; we had helped open the YMCA; our work was done. We promised to come back to Tobago often and volunteer with the YMCA, and we continue to do so.

We left after a wonderful going-away party at the YMCA with staff and friends and arrived back in Toronto in time for Christmas.

We found out the person who had attacked and robbed us twice had been arrested and convicted of another assault and robbery and had gone to jail for a very long time.

Joanne and I reflect from time to time on the three years in Tobago working with the community, making friends, and helping open a YMCA. We have concluded that the two unfortunate incidents, although traumatic, did not diminish the more powerful life-enriching experience we had.

And the Y pool has had a lasting impact. Following the opening of the pool, with its demonstrated success, we approached the Tobago House of Assembly with a proposal that we called Every Child a Swimmer.

The Division of Education, Youth Affairs, and Sport agreed that swimming would be incorporated into the elementary school curriculum, with children being bussed to the Y weekly for swim lessons. The Tobago House of Assembly provided the funding, and the parents contributed to the transportation costs. It gave us great pride to see approximately 1,200 kids a week learning to swim on the island.

Our time spent in Tobago gave us great joy. We made many friends among our Aqua Jogging group and others. Friends came to visit from Canada. We travelled up island and visited the small villages and extraordinary beaches in Castara, Englishman's Bay, and Pirates Cove.

Our favourite place, though, was Parlatuvier. One day Joanne and I picked up an elderly man hitchhiking. His name was Harold Glasgow and he was heading home to Parlatuvier. After that we would visit him and his wife often. His son Andy owns the local bar overlooking Parlatuvier Bay. This may be the most beautiful view in the world. Andy's parents have passed away now, and I spoke at his mom's funeral.

Each time we go back to Tobago, we visit Andy at the bar and marvel at the grand view.

Parlatuvier Bay from Andy's Bar.

Our dear neighbour was Luise Kimme. She was an artist originally from Germany and trained in New York. She was a highly respected artist, selling her work throughout the world. She would come by our place in the early morning and we would go to aqua fitness together.

She built an extraordinary house overlooking the Caribbean Sea. Every corner was full of her bronze and wood sculptures as well as her paintings. She loved Tobago and took inspiration for her art from the many local Tobago myths and legends. Her museum, as she called it, was open on Sundays, and we took all our friends there. Sadly, she passed away a few years ago.

Our friend Lloyd McKell in front of Kimme Museum.

Luise Kimme at her studio.

The big difference from Toronto, though, was our dinner parties.

We never went to restaurants or the big hotels. Too expensive. Leave those to the tourists.

Joanne, who had never cooked during all our years in Toronto, learned to cook from our dear friend Ricardo Smith, and we entertained more than we had throughout our marriage. The food, of course, was excellent but what resonates with us still is how we laughed and laughed. Joanne enjoyed the cooking so much that she enrolled in George Brown College's Chef School as a full-time student when we moved back to Toronto!

We also re-created our Christmas Carol Sing and invited everyone, including all our Aqua Jogger friends. People in Tobago love to sing and, being devoutly Christian, particularly love Christmas and carol singing, so the event was a huge hit each year. Joanne and Ricardo cooked up a storm, and the Aqua Joggers donated pastelles, a Christmas favourite in Tobago.

We will always remember Barack Obama being elected on November 4, 2008. That night, Tobagonians took to the street in excitement.

Having been politicians ourselves, we were fascinated by the politics. We realized early on that on a small island it was important to stay neutral at election time.

That said, Joanne and I thought it would be interesting to watch a local political rally. The party in power, the PNM, was running for re-election and most of the people wore red T-shirts. We, of course, did not.

There was an energy to the evening with music, dancing, and speeches. The next day we got several calls pointing out that we had been at the rally. I asked how they knew we had been there, as we had kept a low profile. The answer was simple: We were the only white people there! So no more campaign rallies for us.

Each year from 2011 to 2016, we visited Tobago to see friends and continue our relationship with the YMCA. Most of the visits were short, but each time we felt the better for the visit, and we were inspired by the work of the YMCA.

We decided in 2017 to spend a month back in Tobago. We did aqua fitness each morning under palm trees, I found some table-tennis buddies, and we worked to strengthen the new YMCA Board of Management. We met with newly elected government officials, and we watched the incredible swim team, the Tobago Aqua Warriors, train.

On our last day, we attended the YMCA awards ceremonies. It was a magical time. Proud kids, proud parents, and proud staff.

We returned home to Toronto realizing that the YMCA and the people of Tobago will be part of us for the rest of our lives — and knowing that the Y will continue to have an impact on the local community.

Harmony Movement

In early 1994, Dr. Joseph Wong called, expressing deep concern about the state of race relations in our city. There had been several disturbing incidents in Toronto and across the country. I have learned over the years that when Joseph calls it is best to say yes. He is an impassioned and committed volunteer, taking on a myriad of important causes. And I always know that, however hard I am working, he is always working harder. And he is my family doctor.

We called our mutual friend Mary Anne Chambers, who had worked with us back in my United Way days. Mary Anne had grown up in Jamaica, immigrated to Canada, and had risen to increasingly senior positions at Scotiabank. She later became a member of the provincial government and a cabinet minister.

We felt if we could bring people together from different backgrounds and ethnicities we could accomplish great things. We decided to call ourselves the Harmony Movement, with an emphasis on promoting and celebrating diversity. We wanted to be a nimble enough organization that we could tackle incidents of injustice quickly and effectively by speaking out and advocating.

For me, it was seeing an interview on TV of an older white gentlemen coming out of a legion hall, lamenting the fact that the legions had moved to accept as members Sikhs who had fought in the Second World War. It was a controversial decision, with many opposed to extending membership to what he called "these turban-wearing outsiders." He said, "It's us versus them now." I was left wondering who is *us* and who is *them*. Seemed to me, except for Indigenous people, we are all immigrants to Canada.

The following year, Carol Bell, the deputy mayor of Markham, came out expressing concerns about the growth of "Asian malls" with signs in Chinese. She stated that there were too many Chinese people in Markham. Some of her constituents supported her. But for many others, particularly in the Chinese community, this was racism raising its ugly head yet again.

We all remembered the *W5* episode "Campus Giveaway" with the subtitle "Why the Chinese Are Taking Our Places at the University."

There were community meetings to raise concerns about Carol Bell's statements. Joseph Wong and I went off to meet with Markham Mayor Don Cousens, who we both knew and liked. The meeting did not go well. He expressed the view that was this was no big thing, that it would soon pass, and that Carol Bell was a good person.

We left angry and upset and more determined than ever to do something.

We learned that this "no big thing" was indeed big. The story was carried in the Hong Kong press, saying that Chinese immigrants were no longer welcome in Markham.

The Harmony Movement stepped into this. It was time to use our networks, and we did. We got in touch with the heads of Toronto's major banks. They understood the positive impact of Asian investment. We reached out to Barbara Hall, the mayor of Toronto, and Hazel McCallion, the mayor of Mississauga.

They agreed that something needed to be done, and quickly. They went out and garnered support from other mayors.

The idea was to put together a full-page advertisement, signed by many community organizations, the mayors in the Greater Toronto and surrounding area, and the major banks, welcoming immigrant groups to the Toronto area. By implication, this ad was telling Carol Bell she was wrong. The day before the ad was to go, Brian Davis, a senior official with the Royal Bank, called Mayor Don Cousens to let him know this ad was coming and offering him the opportunity to sign on. He declined. Big mistake.

The full-page ad, sponsored by the Harmony Movement, came out in the *Toronto Star* on a Saturday. Just imagine! The cross section of groups that signed the ad included the Urban Alliance on Race Relations, the Black Action Defence Committee, the Bank of Montreal, community leaders, and twelve area mayors. A powerful coalition indeed.

By Monday the tide had turned. Carol Bell did go quiet and was rarely heard from again. Don Cousens changed his position quickly.

Today, Markham is Canada's most diverse city. Marcus Gee, a writer with the *Globe and Mail*, put it this way in a column a few years ago:

> It seems a long time ago ... when deputy mayor Carole Bell made headlines and angered the Chinese community ... by complaining about all the Asian malls that were going up.
>
> The municipal government positively boasts of the city's changed complexion ... The benefits of diversity, it says, "are obvious; where else can one walk — in the malls, recreation centres, parks, schools, streets — and enjoy the pleasures and wisdom of so many traditions all at once? Markham is directly connected, through ties of history and family, to every corner of our globalized world.

As for the Harmony Movement, Cheuk Kwan, the extraordinary, long-serving executive director, has built a strong staff and board of directors. They continue to engage Canadians in schools and social service settings across the country.

Their mandate: "We empower youth to become leaders for social change by implementing diversity education in schools and communities." He has built a powerful, youth-led organization that works to change attitudes through education.

Their track record is compelling. Joseph, Mary Anne, and I are only peripherally involved now. The next generation has taken charge. That is as it should be.

Brothers

I grew up with two younger brothers, Bill and Jim. Bill was only fifteen months younger, but quickly surpassed me in all sports except table tennis. Bill was a larger-than-life person ... popular, talented, and engaging. He was a good student and a tremendous athlete. With his silky-smooth swing, he emerged as one of the two best junior golfers in Ontario.

He was popular with his fellow students at Lawrence Park Collegiate and went on to study at Victoria College at the University of Toronto. He joined the Delta Kappa Epsilon Fraternity on St. George Street and lived there for a time.

He did not graduate and started into the workforce. For reasons we could not understand, he kept losing jobs. He moved into our apartment on Ontario Street. One weekend in the spring of 1969, he was with his buddies in Montreal and came home completely wasted. Obviously, he had been on drugs.

We took him to Sunnybrook Hospital, where he was admitted to the psychiatric ward. He stayed there for several weeks, coming home to our place on weekends. But rather than getting better, he seemed to be more depressed. One weekend, he came to our apartment for a visit and presented me with a list he had made: "Reasons to live and reasons to die." I was badly shaken by this, and I tried to reach his psychiatrist. I did not succeed.

That evening, my beautiful brother Bill opened the window of the third floor of his hospital ward, stood on the ledge, and jumped. He did not die, but as the hospital person who called us at 10:00 p.m. said, "We believe he is brain dead." The family gathered, as families do, and cried and cried. To this day, I remember my poor mother wailing in her grief. We decided that it was best to let Bill go and donate his organs to others.

A few hours later, I had to go down and identify the body. A few days later, we had the funeral and Bill was buried in a grave beside his grandparents at the Mount Pleasant Cemetery. Had this happened today, I am sure there would have been an inquest to determine how a young person in the psychiatric ward, known to be suicidal, could have died this way. Back then, though, we met with the hospital officials and Dr. Ronald Billings, psychiatrist at Sunnybrook, and tried our best to understand what had happened. Looking back, we probably should have asked some hard questions. So focused on our grief, we did not.

Our family tried our best to get back to normal. It was not easy. My mom and my younger brother, Jim, took it the hardest. Bill was twenty-four when he died. Jim was in his last year of high school.

Jim was also a great athlete, president of the Athletic Board at Lawrence Park Collegiate, popular with his fellow students, and handsome too. What we did not know then, because Jim did not tell us till much later, was that he had been sexually abused many times when he first started high school by a high-profile member of Rosedale Golf Club. When Jim was fourteen, Tim Chisholm, now deceased, took him during March Break to his place in Florida. Jim came back with lots of gifts and new clothing.

Over the next couple of years, Tim Chisholm invited many young teenagers to his home and to his cottage on an island in Muskoka. Most of the kids liked it a lot, as it meant free beer and steaks. But there would always be one or two who were vulnerable. I feel certain that Jim was not the only person Tim Chisholm abused. Sadly, many of Tim's friends and colleagues knew what he was up to and turned a blind eye. It is my firm belief that were this to happen today, Tim Chisholm would be in jail for a very long time.

Jim went on to the University of Western Ontario and graduated. He was also an outstanding golfer and had spent his summers working at the Ontario Golf Association. He was headed for a career there, but soon after he, like our brother Bill, seemed unable to hold a job. He drove a van out west and spent time skiing and working at the Banff Springs Hotel. When he came home, he had a complete breakdown and was admitted to the Clarke Institute of Psychiatry.

Over the next few months, he went through many tests and was eventually diagnosed with schizophrenia. Times were different then, and treatment was pretty random. Jim went through a variety of different treatments, including electroshock therapy, different drugs, mega vitamin therapy, and so forth. He lived on a farm for a while, in an apartment with three other patients, and finally came back home to live with our parents, who loved him. He couldn't get a full-time job, but volunteered downtown at Central Neighbourhood House, helping with the Stroke Club and the Home Help Programme. He also volunteered at the Career Centre at the University of Toronto. He takes his medication, which helps to stabilize him and to reduce the hearing of voices common to people with schizophrenia.

He moved into St. George House, supportive housing run by Loft Community Services. His old high school buddies still invite him back every year to play in the annual Paint Pot Golf Tournament (some of them had summer painting jobs in university). Two friends, Ron Gray and Drew Belshaw, visit from time to time. Jim's life is okay. When the kids were growing up he would come over to our house once a week and play table tennis, often doubles with Joseph and Keith.

In the fall of 2000, I got a call from Healthy Minds Canada, then the Canadian Psychiatric Research Foundation, asking me to make the keynote speech at their annual luncheon to talk about our family and mental health. I am not certain why. Though I was becoming known as an inspirational speaker, I had not shared our family's personal story. I thought about it and decided that, if my brother Jim was comfortable with the idea, I would do it.

Jim said, "If it helps people, do it." A few days before the speech, a reporter from the *Toronto Star* called saying that they wanted to do a feature story about me and my brother. Around that time, Michael Wilson, the former federal minister of finance, had spoken publicly about his son Cameron's battle with depression and his suicide. He did it to help break the stigma of mental illness, and the *Star* thought my story would do the same. (It has been alleged that Michael Wilson's son Cameron was one of those abused by Tim Chisholm.)

I asked Jim again, and he agreed, so then I called my mother. My father had passed away a couple of years earlier, and Mom was living in a retirement home at 4 Teddington Park. She was appalled. She said, "Dear, do not do this. We keep this story to ourselves." I tried every way I could to get her onside, but it did not work. She was from a different era, one in which such family tragedies were not shared.

But I had agreed to give the speech, and the next day, I did tell our family story at the luncheon. It was very personal. The speech was well received. One of the people attending was Michael Wilson. He came over to chat, congratulated me on the speech, and inquired if there was anything he could do to be helpful. I blurted out, "Call my mother!"

He did. Later that evening I got a call from my mom. She said, "Dear, I got a call from Michael Wilson tonight. He is a Tory, you know." My mom was a Conservative. I am not. She went on to say, "He made a lot of sense. I am proud of what you did today. Now, get me thirty copies of the article in the *Toronto Star* tomorrow — I want to give it to all the residents in the retirement home." Again, the lesson learned: "If you can't do it yourself find someone who can."

Jim and I continue to play golf from time to time and we regularly play table tennis. A few years back, he won the long drive competition at the annual Paint Pot Tournament. He has never lost his golfing ability and can still hit a long ball.

One March, I took Jim down to Pinehurst, North Carolina, over the Easter weekend to play golf. We flew down to Raleigh, rented a car, drove to Pinehurst, stayed in a nearby motel, and had two fabulous days playing golf.

On Easter Sunday, when we got up, Jim said he did not feel like playing golf that day, leaving me wondering what we should do. It struck me that maybe going to church for Easter would be a good idea. Jim agreed. Then the question was where to go. I was looking up Episcopal Churches in the phone book (the equivalent of Anglican in Canada), when this strikingly handsome Black man in an amazing white suit walked into the lobby.

I went up to him and asked if he was going to church. He said he was. I then asked if it was okay for us to join him, and I noted that we only had casual clothes. He said simply, "You are always welcome in the house of the Lord — follow me."

We arrived at this small wooden church on the outskirts of town. We were the only white people there. It turned out that this man was the minister, and before the service, he invited us into the small back room where we met with the elders of the Church.

The conversation was going along quite nicely, but Jim, as often happened, was quiet in the group. Just before the service was to start, the minister turned to me and said, "Brother Gordon, would you lead us in prayer?" I panicked. I am a good public speaker, but I was not up for this at all! I'm not quite sure how it happened, but I had the sense that Jim could do this well. Jim always said the grace at family dinners. I turned to Jim and said, "Jim, why don't you lead the prayer?" Well, he did, and he was fantastic.

We then all went into the church service. The music was inspiring and uplifting. The minister had people clapping and saying "halleluiah" loudly. We were welcomed and introduced to the congregation. It was a service that we will not ever forget.

As we were leaving, I was walking down the corridor with the minister. He noted that my brother Jim was quite quiet all morning except when he led the prayer and asked me why that was. To be honest, I had no idea. He startled me a bit by saying, "Do you think Jim spoke so confidently when he led the prayer because we all had our eyes closed?" The idea had never occurred to me. No one who had ever worked to help Jim had mentioned this idea either.

The minister then suggested that it might be easier for Jim if I did not look him straight in the eye when talking with him. That night we went out for dinner and I tried it out, looking slightly away from him as I talked. Jim talked more to me that night than he had in a long time. I continue that approach to this day. I am not a very religious person, but the phrase, "the Lord works in mysterious ways" seems appropriate. We went back to that church the following two years on Easter. I made, for me, a sizable donation.

Five years ago, Jim began complaining of severe back pain, which resulted in his doctor, Dr. Joseph Wong, ordering several tests. It turned out that Jim had a serious back infection that led to major surgery. Due to his mobility problem, Loft transferred him to one of their seniors' buildings, St. Anne's Place. He has his own room and has gotten involved with the church next door, where he often reads the lesson. We still play Ping-Pong together. Jim, in his seventies, is still in the game, and I admire his remarkable courage every day. Our family is the better for having Jim in our lives.

Table Tennis Is My Great Joy and Passion

When I was young, my dad taught me how to play on the table in our small basement. The ceiling was low and there was little room to back up. Dad just said, "Keep the ball in play." He used to give me big handicaps, like 15 points; in those days the game was to 21. We played hard, I got better, and gradually Dad lowered my handicap.

Boyhood friends, like Bill Baker, Roger Steele, and Bruce Armstrong, would come over and we would play by the hour. One of my friends, Ron Wisman, who lived on top of the paint store his father owned on Yonge Street, was very good. His sister was a provincial champion. He encouraged me to play competitively. My dad encouraged me to focus on being really good at one sport.

So off I went at age twelve to play in my first junior tournament, organized by the *Toronto Star* for young people eighteen and under. I played well, finished second, and was ready for more.

I played and played and played. I was successful, winning my share of junior tournaments both citywide and provincially and was the Ontario Junior Men's Champion for four years in a row.

A disclaimer here is in order. The number of competitive players was small in those days!

One of my summer jobs was at the National Life Insurance company. They put me on their team, which competed in the Financial Table Tennis League.

Table tennis was not high profile then, nor is it to this day in Canada, but at my high school, Lawrence Park, the football team had a table in the dressing room and the players would invite me down to play.

When I went to Trinidad in the sixties, I continued to play competitively and won the Trinidad B Division title. In Chicago, when I was in college, I did well in the school tournaments and played in a couple of citywide events.

Joanne and I had a table in our basement when our boys were growing up, and we would often play, particularly doubles with my brother. It was a great family time. But my competitive days seemed long past.

A couple of times on family holidays, there was a local tournament, and I would find that fierce competitive spirit return, usually winning first prize — a bottle of local rum!

One evening I was at an event at Heather Munro-Blum's house. She was the dean of social work at U of T when I was there. I got talking to her husband, Len Blum, a well-known movie producer and writer. Somehow the discussion turned to table tennis, and he suggested we leave the party and go down to his basement to play. Down we went.

This was a huge basement with high ceilings and lots of room behind each end of the table. I noted he had a robot machine. I said to myself, *This guy is serious*, and he was. We played and had a very good time.

He asked what I did on Thursday mornings. I noted that I worked then.

He suggested that I come over at 8:00 a.m. to play. And we did. It was fantastic! I was about to rush away when he suggested we have a sauna and a shower. The idea of slowing down had never occurred to me. But he was right — it felt like older guys playing in the sandbox again. I got to work a little late, but I suspect I was more productive.

I did this almost every week for a year. I used to put in my calendar at work "meeting with Dr. Len Blum." I think my staff thought I was meeting with a psychiatrist, so they never asked. As for me, if this was a form of therapy, it certainly worked!

When we lived in Tobago for three years, we bought a table and I had a wonderful time playing with various excellent players.

Back in Toronto, we moved into an apartment and had no room for a table-tennis table. Then SPIN opened at Spadina and King. Actress Susan Sarandon was an early investor in SPIN, a night-club-type venue with table tennis as its focus. It started in New York and was spreading to other major cities. In the evenings, people partied there and played a little table tennis. But in the afternoons and on weekends, people came just to play table tennis.

Our family started to go on Sundays. We would take turns playing and have lunch. Jim always came with us, and sometimes our friend John Piper would join us. We were having a good time. I entered a couple of small tournaments there and did quite well.

But then a new world opened to me when I went to the Hot Docs Festival and saw an astonishing movie simply titled *Ping Pong*. It followed eight senior citizen players to the world Veterans Table Tennis championship in China in 2012, where over 3,000 people competed. In 2016, over 4,800 people competed in Spain.

This movie inspired me to get better! I often wondered, had I pursued table tennis in a serious way at age eighteen, how well would I have done? I decided to get back in the game in a serious way.

I looked for a table-tennis club to join and found My Table Tennis Club in Mississauga, where older people played during the day.

Off I went and made some new friends. Almost all were of Chinese origin, with a group originally from Hong Kong and another originally from mainland China. They made me feel welcome.

The game had changed a lot. It was more offensive and much faster. The game is now to 11 points, not 21.

I started to go twice a week and found myself often with Sandy Chu, who knew everybody at the club and operated as the unofficial social convenor. We got to talking about competitive table tennis. He has won many tournaments in his age division (he is now in his eighties) and he recommended that if I really wanted to discover how well I could do at the competitive level in my age group, I should head to China.

Sandy had a good friend, Bill Chan, who spoke fluent English and lived in Shijiazhuang (about two hours from Beijing by bullet train), a hotbed of table tennis. Bill had lived in Canada and the United States but had settled down in Shijiazhuang and was deeply involved in table tennis as both player and translator. His wife is a full-time table-tennis coach.

So off I went for fourteen days of table-tennis training, six hours a day. This is the blog of my trip: https://cressyinchina.wordpress.com. And here is what I learned…

The Chinese are the best in the world for a reason. The players start younger, train longer, and work harder than anyone else. The Chinese government provides significant resources for youth development.

I played with young people, sixteen to eighteen years of age. They were utterly fantastic. Most of them have been playing six hours a day, six days a week for over six years. They are beyond fit, and their strokes are smooth and forceful. Their footwork is amazing. Clearly, I was not in their league at all. But they were quite kind to me.

In the afternoon, we would do multi-ball drills. Two hundred balls would come at me one after the other and quite fast. I would practise forehand smash and then backhand smash. Then forehand and backhand combined. The key was to get the stroke smooth and consistent. We did this day after day. Mind you, the juniors have been doing it day after day and month after month and year after year.

In the early evening, I would play with my fellow seniors and have a very good time. Although I did not speak the language, we found the thumbs-up symbol worked very well. For a couple of days, they had me focus on serves and serve returns, with an emphasis on spinning the ball. When I went back to my quite spartan hotel in the evening, I was a mixture of tired and energized.

The head coach said I was improving, and I was, but — and here is the kicker — he suggested to really move to the next level I would need to come for the three-month programme. That was a nonstarter!

As I left Shijiazhuang, I spent time in Beijing visiting Tiananmen Square, the Forbidden City, and the Great Wall. Then I said goodbye to my friend Bill Chan, who had looked after me for two weeks, and flew home.

Tiananmen Square. Note the young boy with the peace sign.

Back in Toronto, I was re-energized in table tennis. I found some serious research that showed table tennis is "brain food" for the elderly. Further, playing table tennis is an excellent activity for people with early dementia and Alzheimer's. I went to the Salvation Army seniors' residence, where my friend John Piper lived, and every Thursday I played with a group of seniors. We were having a lot of fun, and they were improving. Their hand-eye coordination got better, as did their stamina. And we laughed a lot. I presented medals to each of the players at Christmastime. The staff, Gail and Carol, thanked me for coming each week.

What I am not sure they understood is that the person having the best time was me. Sadly, during the pandemic, table tennis was stopped.

Back at My Table Tennis Club, I played twice a week until the pandemic closed the club, but I did stay in touch with several of my friends. Some of them told me of anti-Asian abuse they were experiencing due to the pandemic's origins. I did not like this, so I wrote an opinion piece for the *Toronto Star*. I have included my article at the end of this book.

Now I am playing at the Trinity Bellwoods Community Centre, near my home. I have made some new friends.

In October 2023, I participated in the Huntsman World Senior Games in St. George, Utah. There were more than 11,000 athletes competing in thirty-five different sporting events. In table tennis, I won the bronze medal in the Men's Singles Over-80 division. I won the gold medal in the rated division at my level, which is open to both women and men over 50.

The whole experience was exhilarating, stressful, tiring, and exciting all at the same time. The medals are nice and will hang on the wall. But that magic memory is seared into my brain forever.

The Fight to End Carding

Damn It, Do It

Over fifty years ago, as I described earlier, I returned to live in Toronto after Mr. Gleason, the head of the Elliott Donnelley Youth Center in Chicago, advised me, "Take what you learned in Trinidad and the south side of Chicago and see if you can make a difference back home."

I have had the privilege over the last five decades of working with some icons in the Black community. Some are no longer with us: Dudley Laws, Charlie Roach, Wilson Head, Beverly Mascoll, Al Mercury, Herb Carnegie, Stanley Grizzle, Verda Cook, Al Hamilton, Bromley Armstrong, Harold Brathwaite, Lloyd McKell, and the Honourable Lincoln Alexander.

Many, though, are still out there fighting for social justice. People like Denham Jolly, Alvin Curling, Councillor Michael Thompson, Zanana Akande, Mary Anne Chambers, Mark Beckles, Royson James, Trevor Massey, Ken Jeffers, Wes Hall, Donna Harrow, Oji Adisa, Ita Sadu, Bev Salmon, Joan Pierre, Carole Adriaans, Selwyn Pieters, Hamlin Grange, Pamela Appelt, Neil Price, Dwight Drummond, Jean Augustine, Afua Cooper, and many more. As important, a new generation of Black community leaders is emerging.

I have had the privilege to march, to protest, and to celebrate with many of these leaders. Some of the work has been outlined earlier in this book.

Advances have been made. Many Black Canadians have risen to significant positions in business, education, politics, and labour. Despite many achievements, however, there is still a significant struggle for racial equality.

One of the biggest problems is the practice of "carding" or "racial profiling." As was clearly documented in 2002 by the *Toronto Star* investigative series "Race and Crime," year after year, Black people, particularly young Black men, are disproportionately stopped and carded by police.

This issue has been raised eloquently, forcefully, and sometimes angrily for many years by members of the Black community.

In the 2014 municipal election, many Black leaders were conflicted between supporting Olivia Chow or John Tory. Both had worked extensively in the Black community. In the last couple of weeks of the campaign, the mayoralty race began to tighten, with Olivia's support slipping, and Doug Ford emerging stronger. Many leaders in the Black community came out publicly for John Tory, including former provincial Cabinet Ministers Mary Anne Chambers, Alvin Curling, and Zanana Akande. They had high hopes that John Tory would finally do the right thing on carding.

After John Tory was elected mayor, he chose to sit on the Police Services Board, displacing Councillor Michael Thompson as the mayor's appointee. Michael, the one Black member of City Council, had served effectively on the Police Services Board during the previous term and had led the push to end the practice of carding. Michael was furious.

There was a perception that Mayor Tory was too cozy with the Police Union, which strongly supported carding. When a watered-down proposal on carding was passed by the Police Services Board, the Black community was enraged and said so on social media, in the press, especially in SHARE newspaper, at the Police Services Board, and in the community. Enough was enough.

At the same time, *Toronto Life* magazine featured an article by journalist Desmond Cole. On the front cover was a black-and-white picture of Cole with the headline "The Skin I'm In: I've Been Interrogated By the Police More Than 50 Times — all Because I'm Black." His article had an impact on a lot of people, including me.

I met with my old friend Ken Jeffers, a longtime activist and recently retired city employee, and Donna Harrow, the head of the Alexandra Park Community Centre. We were talking about forming a group of "elders" who might come together with one voice to speak out on some of the critical issues of the day. Obviously, the carding issue was front and centre.

On May 21, 2015, I attended the Tommy Douglas Institute at George Brown College, entitled "Education & Activism: Rethink, Resist, Reclaim." The organizers were from the Community Worker Programme, which was celebrating its fortieth anniversary. I knew some of them from earlier times, and I wanted to listen to Chris Hedges, the keynote speaker.

In the afternoon, there was a panel discussion featuring Desmond Cole, who I had never met, and Ausma Malik, a recently elected school trustee of the Muslim faith. I knew her quite well, as she had run a joint campaign with my son Joe as he ran successfully for City Council.

They made a compelling case to act now.

When it came time for questions, I rose, not to ask a question but to say that we attendees should take collective action. There was polite applause. At the end of the session, one of the students came up to me and said, "You said we should do something." I responded by saying, "Yes, I did." Then she looked me straight in the eye and simply said, "Well then, damn it, do it!"

That was it for me — I was back.

I was reminded of Eldridge Cleaver's line in his book *Soul on Ice*: "Not to act — is to act."

I went home and talked with Joanne. She was, and is to this day, passionate about the issue of racial equality. She had worked for three years in Chingola, in the Copperbelt in Northern Zambia, in the mid-1970s, teaching women skills to help them get well-paid jobs in the copper mines. She and I first met when she was working on the staff of the Urban Alliance on Race Relations. As a vice president of the Centre for Addiction and Mental Health (CAMH), she led its major organizational change initiative to instill diversity practices in all parts of CAMH. She hired the formidable Kwasi Kafele to work with her. They were an epic team — together they made things happen.

We decided that we had to do something and connected with several Black leaders to see how they viewed the situation. They were extremely upset and felt let down, betrayed by John Tory. Mary Anne Chambers was perhaps the most forceful. She had tried to get through to Mayor Tory on the phone but was blocked by a senior aide. Apparently, this aide told her that the only people concerned about the carding were "you people." He was upset with the articles by Royson James in the *Star* that attacked the mayor for his position on carding, and he suggested Mary Anne call Royson James and tell him to back off.

I had a lunch on Tuesday, May 26, with Ken Jeffers, Donna Harrow, and two people from the George Brown Community Worker Programme, Resh Budhu and Neil Price. We all agreed that the time to act was now.

We talked to several of our friends, leaders in the Black community, who agreed to serve as senior advisors, including Zanana Akande, Jean Augustine, Mary Anne Chambers, Alvin Curling, and Councillor Michael Thompson.

Then we went to work preparing a statement: "Stop Carding Now."

Stop Carding Now

A growing group of prominent citizens is speaking out against the police practice of carding. We are committed to a Toronto that is inclusive, diverse, welcoming, and respectful, and carding does not fit that vision.

Carding has led many in our city to distrust and disrespect our police. Anger, hurt and unrest have replaced any benefits police may derive from this practice.

We all need to oppose carding vehemently. We resent having to witness its debilitating impact on our neighbours. It sends a message of hopelessness to young people with black or brown skin. We cannot and will not accept this for any group or community in our city. We do not need a new generation of Torontonians growing up to believe our police are their adversaries.

We are offended by the notion of casually and routinely stopping citizens, outside of police investigations of actual criminal acts that have occurred, to question and record, and then store personal data in police files. We are deeply distressed that Toronto residents of colour are subjected to this invasion of their privacy when the overwhelming majority of white-skinned citizens are not.

We believe that carding violates the human rights of citizens. It goes against the principles of our Charter Rights. It paints a disturbing picture and repeats a narrative that is reminiscent of ugly practices that were historically endured by racialized residents, particularly those of African Canadian backgrounds.

We cannot allow an environment of anger and distrust of our police to exist and fester in our city, particularly among the African Canadian and other racial minority communities. We cannot sit back and allow this to undermine everything we teach our children about Canada being a fair and equal society.

We urge Mayor John Tory, Alok Mukherjee, Chair of the Police Services Board and Mark Saunders, Chief of Police to immediately cease the practice of carding. And we call on all citizens of this city to step forward and make known their distaste of this fear-mongering practice.

Our call is not intended to interfere with the common police practice of conducting criminal investigations in order to apprehend criminals in the interest of public safety. Rather, it seeks to correct an injustice that harms police/community relations, and damages the reputation of our police service and the city it serves.

If this demeaning practice of selected carding is not terminated quickly, it will irreversibly divide and separate our various communities and cultures. We must be a city where every citizen is treated equally and justly.

Stop carding now

We called our group Concerned Citizens to End Carding, and we began to call around to get a broad base of support for the statement.

The response was quick, decisive, and encouraging. Most said, "Count me in." Here is a list of some of our prominent supporters:

- three former mayors: David Crombie, Barb Hall, and John Sewell
- three former heads of the United Way: Anne Golden, Francis Lankin, and me
- two former directors of education: Harold Brathwaite and Joan Greene

- two former members of the Police Services Board: Dr. Gordon Chong and Roy Williams
- three university presidents: Sheldon Levy, Meric Gertler, and Sarah Diamond
- lawyers, business and community leaders, including the following: David McCamus, Denham Jolly, Noella Milne, Warren Seyffert, Ken Jeffers, Robert Wright, Peter Oliver, Allan and Judy Broadbent, Donna Hill, Dr. David Bell, Diana Bennett, Joanne Campbell, Jean Cuddy, Merle Grant, Spencer Lanthier, Dorothy Shoicht, and Howard Morton
- educators: Lloyd McKell, Penny Milton, Walter Pitman, and Kamala Jean Gopie
- authors and journalists: Joy Fielding and Michelle Lansberg
- heads of community organizations: Donna Harrow, Max Beck, Zeib Jeeva, Ratna Omidvar, J. Doughas Salmon, Dr. Joseph Wong, Cheuk Kwan, and Warren Salmon
- former city councillors: David Socknacki and Bev Salmon
- a former Canadian ambassador to the United Nations and chair of the Stephen Lewis Foundation: Stephen Lewis
- a past CEO of YMCA of Greater Toronto: Henry Labatte
- a former CEO of CAMH: Paul Garfinkel
- a magician: David Ben
- a former attorney general of Ontario: Roy McMurtry
- an EVP of public affairs for Edelman and co-chair of Mayor John Tory's campaign: Bob Richardson

By anyone's assessment, this was not a group to be ignored.

We set a time for a press conference at City Hall on Thursday, June 7, at 11:00 a.m. and agreed to meet beforehand in Councillor Michael Thompson's office.

We put out a news release on the following Wednesday, and things started to happen — and happen fast. Word got around quickly. More people wanted to sign up. Matt Galloway called for an interview on *Metro Morning*. At first, I thought they were calling to ask my son Joe, the city councillor, for an interview, as he is on all the time!

Early that evening, I received a call at home from John Tory. He was clearly very unhappy about this. John and I go way back, and although we come from different political backgrounds, we always got along.

The conversation did not go well, as he felt blindsided by our initiative.

I let him know in no uncertain terms that part of the problem here was that people who supported him in the public during the campaign had felt let down and let down badly. I told him the story of Mary Anne Chambers. He was shocked.

He asked if a small group would meet him early in the morning. Anne Golden, Mary Anne Chambers, and I met on Thursday morning with John Tory and his chief of staff, Chris Ebey. Mark Saunders, the new police chief was out of town and participated by phone. The chair of the Police Services Board, Alok Mukherjee, an old friend from my school board days, attended. Little was accomplished, as we were not interested in simply hearing justifications for the existing policy on carding.

Then we went down to Councillor Michael Thompson's office for a short reception before the press conference. The atmosphere was electric. Although we had no idea if the media or the public would show up, there was a feeling that something very special was about to occur.

The organizing committee.

We walked down the corridor to the press conference. The media was there in large numbers. So was the public.

Press Conference, June 7, 2015.

Michael Thompson welcomed people and said it was time to end carding.

Barbara Hall, former Toronto mayor and recently retired head of the Ontario Human Rights Commission, gave a fiery speech. Mary Anne Chambers recalled her anguish as a Black mother raising children, fearing every day for their safety during encounters with the police.

But the most powerful speaker was the wise and revered Roy McMurty, Ontario's former attorney general, who clearly and dispassionately made the case to end carding. Basically, he said carding was unconstitutional and it was time to end the practice permanently.

Another seminal moment was when one of the media asked the assembled crowd, "Who here has been carded?" Not a single white person put up their hand but virtually everyone else in the room did.

We followed up with an online petition to stop carding, which quickly had 7,000 signatures.

Three days later, John Tory held a press conference saying that he was going to end carding permanently.

A week later, Neil Price wrote an article in *Now Magazine* titled "Who Really Killed Carding." He talked about me at length. He did not tell me about the article in advance and, at first, I was upset about that.

But then I went back to the article and realized that it was really a tribute to the Black activists who had worked on these issues for years. I grew up blissfully unaware of my white privilege. My experiences in Trinidad and Tobago and the south side of Chicago taught me a lot.

Since that time, I have come to know and admire Neil Price. He is a young Black leader who is beginning to make his mark.

I would like to say that carding ended there. The province got into the act and said there was no place in Ontario for carding. This initiative shifted the focus from the Toronto Police Services Board, in many ways letting it off the hook. Then hearings were held, and a new set of regulations proclaimed. Then it was back to police services boards across the province for implementation. Many remain unhappy and discouraged, as carding remains, but with more restrictions.

Did we end carding? No, but I think that we are in a better spot than we were before.

But — and this is a big *but* — young Black males are still targeted by the police.

We still have much work to do.

Still Listening, Still Learning

Each of us must look at what drives us forward each day. For me that starts with positive energy and a positive attitude. I begin the day by saying "I am fantastic." I tell others that all day long. Not just "I am fine" or "I am okay" or "I am not bad."

Being an upbeat person works for other people too. It is contagious. I have taught my kids to do this too.

My son Keith is a superb Special Education specialist at Essex Public School in Toronto. He taught in Chung Du, China, for two years.

For a couple of summers, to supplement his income, he taught English as a Second Language in the summer at George Brown College to students mostly of Asian origin. He got the students to practise their greetings to other people and to try out the expression "I am fantastic."

One day when I was at work at George Brown College, I went out for lunch to Burger King, just around the corner. I know I should not go there, from a healthy eating point of view, but the $4.99 Whopper-and-fries special on Tuesdays is hard to resist. I bought my Whopper special and sat down at a small table. I turned to the guy across from me and said, "How are you doing?" He smiled back at me and said in a clear voice, "I'm fantastic." I was blown away. I asked how he came to say that. He said, "My teacher at George Brown told us to try it." He told me it works and always starts a conversation.

I had a special friend in Tobago named Carl Groome. He was on our YMCA steering committee and was a senior official with the Tobago House of Assembly. He had a greeting on his phone that worked for me.

He always started with, "Pleasant good morning to you."

It made me feel good. Amazing how one word in front of "good morning" can do that.

I prefer to always look at the glass as half full. More than that, I believe deeply that things can and will get better. And that we all have a responsibility to be part of the solution. On top of that, I do believe if we miss the joy of it, we miss all of it.

The changes in this city during my lifetime have been profound.

I grew up in a white city. It is no more. The term *visible minority* no longer exists in this city. And the city is profoundly better for it.

Breakthroughs are occurring everywhere.

When the Cressy Leadership awards (described earlier in this book) started back in 1994, the first group was 75 percent Caucasian. In 2019, the Caucasian number was 25 percent.

These are ten life lessons I have learned and described through stories in this book:

1. Take risks, get outside your comfort zone, and be tenacious.
2. Start where people are at.
3. Go out to bring the people in.
4. Take a good idea and make it better.
5. Get the inside onside — before you go outside.
6. If you cannot do it yourself, find someone who can.
7. If it is the right thing to do, find a way to do it.
8. Deeds must outrun words.
9. Bastille storming is not enough.
10. Positive energy carries the day.

What Is Next

For me, turning eighty this year means I have more time to do things.

It means focusing on what is important.

It means keeping deeply connected with family.

It means spending time with people who helped me in earlier times and now are on the downward slope of life.

It means keeping physically active and healthy.

It means being involved in community building.

It means being willing to take a stand.

I have listened. I have learned.

I have tried to follow James Gleason's sage advice from Chicago some fifty years ago, when he told me, "You are not going to make a difference here on the south side of Chicago. Take what you learned in Trinidad and Tobago and here in Chicago and go home to Toronto and make a difference there."

It has been a great run. I choose to play on.

Newspaper Articles

Toronto duo builds public swimming pool in Tobago

Toronto Star
By John Honderich, Former Chair of the Board
Sunday, Sept. 5, 2010

TOBAGO — 'Tis a story told often before — a retired Canadian couple goes abroad to pursue their dream.

Some succeed, but probably many more struggle to make a real difference.

That is why the story of former city councillors Gordon Cressy and Joanne Campbell, who moved to the Caribbean paradise of Tobago, is so particularly striking.

This past weekend, in an often moving and joyous ceremony, they saw the realization of their dream — the opening of Tobago's first-ever public swimming pool.

More than 40 years ago, as a student volunteer with CUSO, Cressy was instrumental in launching Trinidad's first YMCA pool.

Thirty months ago, he and his wife ended decades of public service and community work in Toronto. Cressy, a former school board chair and head of the Learning Partnership, retired from the

Nelson Mandela Children's Fund. Campbell left Toronto's Centre for Addiction and Mental Health.

The pair set out to replicate the feat of four decades ago on the other island of this two-island republic.

What has emerged is a magnificent, eight-lane, 25-metre pool, complete with smartly tiled change rooms and offices that would be the pride of any Canadian city. Only in the tropics, you don't need a roof.

When they took up residence in 2008, they had a few YMCA and other contacts, plus a nest egg of donations from their Toronto friends. But nothing else.

No land. No local money. No knowledge of the local politics.

What they soon discovered is there is no tradition of public philanthropy in Tobago. And the local government had plans for a lavish Olympic-size pool as part of a huge sports complex.

No matter. The duo spent the first six months surveying the scene, feeling out the power brokers and separating the doers from the talkers.

Their goal was to come up with a top-drawer advisory board that would buy the idea and take over the project.

The stroke of genius came in the selection of a chair for the group. It would be Dr. Eastlyn McKenzie, a former senator and star of a former hugely popular Tobago reality show. She is literally an icon of Tobago — and she became the "face" of the project.

Also selected were a preacher, a banker, a restaurateur, a lifeguard and two youth reps, among others. It was striking to see this varied group, resplendent in their new T-shirts, all standing in a line at the official opening. This was their project.

Next, a site. A private donation became unfeasible so Cressy decided to turn directly to the local government, which already had this other plan on its books.

"Imagine," said Tobago's premier, Chief Secretary Orville London, at the opening ceremony.

"Complete newcomers come in and ask for two acres of prime land and $6 million TT ($1 million Canadian)!"

Yet they got it.

Then came the task of raising another $1.2 million to fully finance the project. They did everything from selling topsoil from the excavation site and showing a film of Nelson Mandela to writing untold "begging letters."

Gordon Cressy gives new meaning to the word "relentless," but he does so in a way that produces huge results while raising no offence.

Said the chief secretary: "I have never met a group of people so adept at extracting money."

It would be the banks that finally ponied up to meet the target, Scotiabank included.

Then came the drawings, engineering and contracting. It would be Tobagonian all the way. Again and again the message was simple: this is your project.

The result? A magnificent facility built on time, on budget and totally by Tobagonians.

The official launch drew more than 400 local citizens, which, in an island of only 53,000, is a crowd.

For her speech, McKenzie had been told by Cressy and Campbell to say little about them.

She would have none of it.

For many minutes she extolled their outstanding contribution, concluding: "They taught us what happens when you believe in your dreams."

The crowd then rose in a spontaneous loud standing ovation, leaving the duo completely overwhelmed.

John Honderich is a former publisher of the Toronto Star, and is chair of Torstar's board of directors.

***

Who REALLY killed carding?

How did Gordon Cressy, a white man, help end a racist practice in days that years of black community work had failed to?

Now Magazine
By Neil Price
June 17, 2015

A few days before the memorable press conference convened by Concerned Citizens to End Carding, a colleague and I were invited to lunch at an unremarkable little restaurant on King. The purpose of the lunch was to hear Gordon Cressy's plan to end carding, the police practice of street checks targeting mostly young black and brown men.

What I knew about Cressy was scant: he once led my college's foundation; he was a Toronto city councillor from 1978 to 82; his son Joe is a councillor. That was all.

We arrived to find Cressy and two associates already into their meal. Cressy wore a slightly rumpled blue sports jacket and a pale shirt opened wide at the neck. He has the bronzed skin of a man who spends a fair amount of time outdoors. Across from him sat a bookish woman, her hair in rows of neat plaits. I took a seat opposite a soft-faced gentleman seated beside Cressy.

Cressy, a natural raconteur, spoke animatedly, his fingers dancing lightly along the table's edge. Everyone listened as he regaled us with colourful stories about his time working in Trinidad and Tobago. He seemed to have intimate knowledge of the country, offering a mouthful of lyrics from an obscure calypso.

I was growing restless; I'd come to talk carding. Then Cressy leaned in. "We need to put an end to this thing," he said.

It took me a few seconds to gather that this "thing" was carding. I nodded. Only then did it register that everyone at the lunch was black or brown-skinned except Cressy.

"We've reached a tipping point," he continued, playing with his lightly dressed salad.

I wasn't sure how much Cressy knew about our fight.

He seemed genuinely affronted by the practice. He told us it was Desmond Cole's brilliant essay in Toronto Life in May that moved him to speak out. I was expecting Cressy to offer some suggestion about how to build on all our previous efforts. I wasn't expecting the brutal simplicity of what he had to say.

"We just need to call around and get some people to agree that it's time to end this thing," he said.

I was stunned.

What made him think a few phone calls could achieve what thousands of angry voices hadn't? A hush fell over the table.

Not knowing how else to break the silence, the other guests and I started coughing up the names of people who might speak out. Cressy listened and smiled patiently. "We need people who haven't been speaking out on this yet," he said, his eyes narrowing with what I thought was delight. "Remember, I'm the guy with the Rolodex."

The phrase transported me back to a time when important political decisions were hatched in dimly lit, smoke-filled rooms by the old boys' network. The woman beside me hmm'd. The soft-faced man chuckled.

It was clear that Cressy wasn't talking about the people I knew, but the people he knew - people with power.

"People are saying the black community is fighting this alone," he said. "That's not right." He thumped the table with his fist, scattering some cutlery.

The lunch wasn't a discussion at all - it was a prelude to something more. My head was buzzing with that odd sensation you feel after experiencing something momentous.

Cressy did exactly what he told us he would do. He formed Concerned Citizens to End Carding and called a press conference at City Hall.

I arrived just as the speakers were filing into the space arranged outside the mayor's office. Reporters and photographers were already crushed up against the podium.

There they were, Toronto's power elite, summoned by one of their own in less time than it takes to buy a used car. I had never seen so many influential people in one place. The atmosphere was lively. They laughed and chatted with an air of cozy familiarity. Coming together to make things happen is what they do.

Cressy took the podium.

"We do not want a new generation of youth, particularly black and brown youth, to have to go through this experience," he boomed.

People applauded and whooped.

One by one they took turns speaking to the cameras ringed around them. Heads nodded. The applause grew louder. My chest was taut with emotion.

A few days later, Tory called his own press conference to announce that he'd changed his mind. Carding couldn't be reformed or massaged into respectability after all. That would not be enough. It needed to be exorcised. One side of the city's establishment had sent the message, and the other side received it.

Cressy is a good man. I will always be thankful for what he did that day. There are people in our society who have just as much privilege and choose to remain silent on the issue. Then again, that's what privilege is: having choices. You can choose to act or not. You can choose to care or not. Either way, that privilege continues unimpeded.

While I'm elated that Cressy's decisive action was the impetus that finally cut carding down, I'm perplexed at how often society seems to rely on elites to make change happen. Here was a white man in his twilight years using the influence he still had to end a racist practice. Years and years of community work had failed to do what he did in days. Why?

In the fall I'll return to the classroom, and I'll share the story of my lunch with Gordon Cressy. I'll talk about power and privilege, but I'll also talk honestly about the costs of a life dedicated to community organizing and protest.

I'll remind my students that an activist always runs the risk of working to no avail; that failing to accomplish your dream of social change in your lifetime is more probable than possible. I'll tell them that working from the bottom up is a faith challenge. And that the only thing that keeps you moving along the road to meaningful change is hope.

Gordon Cressy did not kill carding. That credit rightfully belongs to the countless number of people who for decades have fought ceaselessly against excessive policing in Toronto. But the honest truth is, I'm sure as heck glad he dusted off his Rolodex.

Neil Price is executive director of LogicalOutcomes, a non-profit consultancy in Toronto. He is a member of the Tommy Douglas Institute at George Brown College.

***

We must all speak out against anti-Chinese racism

GC
By Gordon Cressy, Contributor
Mon., May 11, 2020 3 min. read

Back in January I was playing table tennis three times a week at My Table Tennis Club in Mississauga. I had returned to playing the game seriously a few years ago. I even went to China to train. The best players in the world come from China. Most of the players at our Club are of Chinese origin, and they have become my friends. We are all "youthful" seniors. What unites us is our love of the game.

During this pandemic the club is obviously closed. The pandemic has impacted all of us, in some unexpected ways. But what has made me angry is the growing anti-Chinese backlash as the COVID-19 virus has dominated our lives. Many of my friends from the club are experiencing this first hand.

I expect there is legitimate concern about how China handled the coronavirus in the early days. But China bashing, egged on by the president of the United State, has allowed, and in some instances, encouraged people to behave inappropriately. This blaming individuals of Chinese origin, and by extension anyone of Asian origin, in our communities is deeply disturbing and unacceptable.

This is what I am hearing from my Chinese Canadian friends ... Sometimes it is subtle, like when people cross the street when a person of Chinese origin is walking near them. Sometimes it is overt, when people say loudly to a person of Chinese origin, "Go back home to where you came from." Other times it is more blatant, like coughing into the face of a person of Chinese origin.

When the police in Vancouver report hateful anti-Asian graffiti on the Chinese Cultural Centre, it becomes open season for attacking people of Chinese/Asian origin. When a federal Conservative leadership candidate questions the loyalty of Canada's brilliant chief public health officer, Dr. Theresa Tam, I want to scream "Stop It."

Many Chinese Canadians are working hard on the front lines of this pandemic as doctors, nurses, and personal support workers. Others have taken up the torch like the Chinese Canadian National Council for Social Justice. These young Chinese Canadians are speaking out against the discriminatory behaviour they are seeing, and they are distributing free hand sanitizers in the community.

A Canadian icon, Dr. Joseph Wong, past Chair of Toronto's United Way and founder of the world renowned Yee Hong Centres for Geriatric Care, is now leading the charge to raise money for protective equipment for front line workers. These front line workers are our support system. Many of them are from Asian heritage.

My message then, is to all of us who are not of Chinese or Asian origin. If we see or hear any of this discriminatory behaviour happening toward our Chinese neighbours or colleagues, let's call it out. Ask them to stop. Let us also be ready to sit down and talk with individuals who have been victims of these attacks.

The Chinese Canadian community should not have to fight this on their own. They are our friends, colleagues and neighbours. Their contributions to this country are enormous. They deserve our support.

We are all in this COVID-19 situation together. Let this not be something that divides us. Playing the blame game does not take us anywhere. Let this experience bring out the best in all of us. We are, as the recent TV special was called, "Better Together."

When this is over, and it will be, I look forward to being back playing table tennis at my club and once again having dim sum lunch with my friends. I hope they will say of us, "You stood up for us when it counted most."

Gordon Cressy is past president of The United Way of Greater Toronto, co-founder of the Nelson Mandela Children's Fund (Canada) and a keen table-tennis player.

***

Gordon Cressy credits T&T for changing his life

Ron Fanfair
December 25, 2016

When Gordon Cressy volunteered for a Canadian University Services Overseas (CUSO) assignment in Trinidad just over five decades ago, little did he envisage the impact he would have in the twin-island republic.

Nearly six weeks after his arrival, the 19-year-old Northern Secondary School part-time janitor was appointed general secretary of the Trinidad YMCA which celebrated its 50th anniversary last Sunday.

He ran a youth hostel, facilitated activities involving various cultural groups and helped establish the island's first public swimming pool in which over 100,000 young people have learned to swim.

Cressy said the two years he spent in Trinidad and the YMCA experience changed his life, spawned his committed to youth work, diversity and equity and motivated him to pursue a fulfilling career in community service.

"I was paid ten Trinidad & Tobago dollars a week along with my lodging which was free," he recalled. "I rode a bicycle, went for roti in St. James and sat in the pit area in the movie theatre. The two years I was there changed my life forever and I am a better person for the whole experience."

Inspired by his initial experience, Cressy – accompanied by his wife Joanne Campbell – went to Tobago six years ago to oversee the construction of the sister -island's first YMCA and community swimming pool. They lived on the island for three years until 2011.

Former Trinidad YMCA president Howard Sabga encouraged Cressy to set up the facility. "He said I should look at it as bookending my career as I started here and I am going to come and finish here," Cressy, who was appointed George Brown College Foundation's president a year ago, said. "Howard also said there was no money to pay me."

Undaunted, Cressy and his wife raised funds in Canada and paid themselves $2,000 a month.

"We went to Tobago and started from scratch," said Cressy who also set up a United Way in T & T. "The first six months, we met people, helped get a board together and got the Tobago House of Assembly to provide us with three acres of land. The government said the facility would cost TT$13 million and they would give us $6 million if we raised the rest."

Through fundraisers and private donations, the first Tobago YMCA and public swimming pool opened in 2010 on time and on budget. Almost 1,200 kids and seniors use the facility weekly.

Though back in Toronto, Cressy and his wife are playing the lead role in the establishment of a second YMCA in Tobago. The facility in Kendal near Roxborough is almost 90 per cent completed.

"We communicate by Skype with the staff there every two weeks and we go down there four times a year to visit," said Cressy, the Nelson Mandela's Children Fund co-founder and Learning Partnership founding chief executive officer. "It will open for summer camp in July."

Cressy, who with his wife own a home in Tobago that they rent out, said the twin-island republic is his spiritual home.

"Guys like Anthony Smart (former T & T attorney general) and Selwyn Ryan (a university professor) came to the University of Toronto for their education," he said. "I could say I went to Trinidad for my education about life, people and things like warmth, kindness and friendliness. It was something quite spectacular and it stayed with me my whole life. It is the place that I look back to as sort of changed the direction of my life."

Cressy's exceptional fundraising skills were again evident at the recent University of the West Indies (UWI) Toronto Benefit Gala when he managed to squeeze a significant sum of money out of entrepreneurs and philanthropists Raymond Chang – the event patron – and Michael Lee-Chin.

Jamaican-born Tessanne Chin, Season 5 winner of the U.S. talent contest, *The Voice*, was not expected to sing at the event where she was recognized with a Luminary Award.

"Ray thought he could get her to do a number and I asked Michael to play along," said Cressy who was the gala's auctioneer. When the bidding stalled at $4,000, Cressy jumped into action. "I asked Michael what was he doing and he joked it was too low," said Cressy.

Lee-Chin then bid $10,000 for Chin to belt out a song and Chang matched it with an addendum – Chin would have to sing a second tune which she did. Lee-Chin offered another $20,000 for Chin to sing a third song.

The net result was $40,000 that will be used to deliver valuable scholarships to UWI students. Yet again, Cressy had come through in a big way for the Caribbean.

Printed in the USA
CPSIA information can be obtained
at www.ICGtesting.com
LVHW012033241123
764837LV00008B/165